# Around the Table

## 52 Essays on Food & Life

**Also by Diana Henry:**

*Crazy Water, Pickled Lemons*
*The Gastropub Cookbook*
*Roast Figs, Sugar Snow*
*Cook Simple*
*The Gastropub Cookbook: Another Helping*
*Food from Plenty*
*Salt Sugar Smoke*
*A Change of Appetite*
*A Bird in the Hand*
*Simple*
*How to Eat a Peach*
*From the Oven to the Table*

# Around the Table

## 52 Essays on Food & Life

DIANA HENRY

MITCHELL BEAZLEY

First published in Great Britain in 2025 by Mitchell Beazley, an imprint of
Octopus Publishing Group Ltd, Carmelite House,
50 Victoria Embankment, London EC4Y 0DZ
www.octopusbooks.co.uk
www.octopusbooksusa.com

An Hachette UK Company
www.hachette.co.uk

The authorized representative in the EEA is Hachette Ireland, 8 Castlecourt Centre, Dublin 15, D15 XTP3, Ireland (email: info@hbgi.ie)

This material was previously published in: *Crazy Water, Pickled Lemons, Roast Figs, Sugar Snow, Food from Plenty, Salt Sugar Smoke, A Bird in the Hand, Simple, How to Eat a Peach* and *From the Oven to the Table*.

Text copyright © Diana Henry 2025

Distributed in the US by Hachette Book Group, 1290 Avenue of the Americas, 4th and 5th Floors, New York, NY 10104

Distributed in Canada by Canadian Manda Group, 664 Annette St., Toronto, Ontario, Canada M6S 2C8

All rights reserved. No part of this work may be reproduced or utilized in any form or by any means, electronic or mechanical, including photocopying, recording or by any information storage and retrieval system, without the prior written permission of the publisher.

Diana Henry has asserted her right to be identified as the author of this work.

ISBN 978-1-84601-600-4
eISBN 978-184601-601-1

A CIP catalogue record for this book is available from the British Library.

Printed and bound in Great Britain.

10 9 8 7 6 5 4 3 2 1

Publishing Director: Alison Starling
Art Director: Juliette Norsworthy
Assistant Editor: Ellen Sleath
Editor: Lucy Bannell
Designer: Matthew Cox at Newman+Eastwood
Cover Artist: Vivienne Williams
Senior Production Manager: Katherine Hockley

This FSC® label means that materials used for the product have been responsibly sourced.

For Claudia Roden, with all my love

# CONTENTS

| | | |
|---|---|---|
| Introduction | | 9 |
| 1. Crazy Water, Pickled Lemons | | 13 |
| 2. Garlic and Liquid Gold | | 19 |
| 3. *Sol o Sombra* | | 27 |
| 4. Pith and Skin | | 35 |
| 5. The Spice Trail | | 43 |
| 6. Around the Table | | 51 |
| 7. Craving Salt | | 57 |
| 8. Hardy Herbs | | 63 |
| 9. Falling in Love with France | | 71 |
| 10. Eggs is Eggs | | 77 |
| 11. The White Stuff | | 81 |
| 12. Heaven Scent | | 89 |
| 13. Watermelon for Breakfast | | 97 |
| 14. Pasta | | 105 |
| 15. After the *Passeggiata* | | 109 |
| 16. I Hated Sunday Lunch | | 115 |
| 17. The Snare of Sugar | | 119 |
| 18. The Streets of San Francisco | | 123 |
| 19. Toast | | 129 |
| 20. Crumbs | | 133 |
| 21. For the Love of Menus | | 135 |
| 22. A Good Bird | | 143 |
| 23. A Barrel of Cukes | | 147 |
| 24. Leftovers | | 151 |
| 25. Soft Herbs | | 155 |
| 26. Summer's End | | 163 |
| 27. Ash Keys and Mangoes on the Roof | | 165 |

| | |
|---|---|
| 28. The Colour Purple | 171 |
| 29. *Tu Veux un Apéritif*? | 177 |
| 30. Hibiscus and Blistered Cobs | 181 |
| 31. From the Hearth | 185 |
| 32. Japanese Lessons | 193 |
| 33. A is for Apple | 197 |
| 34. Soup is Never Dull | 203 |
| 35. Fruits of Longing | 207 |
| 36. October is My Favourite Month | 215 |
| 37. From Russia with Love | 219 |
| 38. I Can Never Resist Pumpkins | 223 |
| 39. The Fat of the Land | 227 |
| 40. The Comfort of Beans | 233 |
| 41. Wild Things | 239 |
| 42. Monsieur Matuchet Plays the Piano | 245 |
| 43. Gathering In | 249 |
| 44. Winter on My Tongue | 255 |
| 45. The Moon and the Bonfires | 261 |
| 46. Carrots and Crows | 267 |
| 47. Crimson Lakes | 275 |
| 48. Ripe and Ready | 283 |
| 49. Marmalade | 289 |
| 50. Sugar Snow | 293 |
| 51. Back Home | 299 |
| 52. Missing New York | 303 |
| **Index** | **312** |
| **Acknowledgements** | **316** |

# INTRODUCTION

This book wasn't planned. I had been asked to record an audio book, containing longer pieces of writing about food from all twelve of my printed books. I had always wanted to record a book, because it is story-telling (reading on *Jackanory* was a childhood dream). When I'd finished planning which pieces should be recorded, and in what order, my editor and I looked at each other and said, at the same time, 'It's a pity this isn't a printed book.'

Though I love recipes (and I really do), it's great to have a book of prose without interruption from ingredients and methods. The essays in these pages cover my whole published life, from my first book, *Crazy Water, Pickled Lemons*, to my most recent, *From the Oven to the Table*. I started writing when my eldest child was eight months old; just as he was approaching two, I took him with me to shoot *Crazy Water* in France. Now he's twenty-seven with a twenty-year-old brother and they've both grown up alongside my books as they were written. In these essays, understandably, I sound a lot younger at the beginning – full of awe and earnestness – than I do now!

The two-and-a-half decades of writing collected here also reveals our recent – and sometimes oddly surprising – kitchen and restaurant history. It's hard to believe that not many people knew what preserved lemons were twenty-five years ago; the explosion of interest in Middle Eastern food was still a little way off. By the time that *From the Oven to the Table* was published, the 'nduja, smoked paprika and burrata that would have been foreign to most of us when I started writing had become commonplace. Whereas once I had taken buses all over London to track down ingredients in specialist shops, now they were all available at the click of a mouse. I'd personally moved from using hexagonal plates – mandatory during the achingly elaborate nouvelle cuisine years – to the stark simplicity in presentation and flavour of Californian cuisine. (Even though people mocked it, joking that the perfect plate of food in San Francisco was a chalky goat's cheese with ripe figs, it had a huge effect, here as well as there.)

I did a lot of travelling, food fads came and went... and my children grew up. I stayed as intrigued by food as ever, using my own books in the kitchen – one of the perks of writing cookbooks is that you gradually collect all your recipes housed between hard covers – and delving into the cooking of new (to me) areas of the world. I explored topics that intrigued me: I wrote about preserving, about making the most of very little, about cooking when it's snowy outside, about drinking apéritifs, about breakfast in Turkey and dinner in Mexico. I am lucky to have spent so much of my life this way. And I have, once you add it all up, probably spent at least a couple of years of that life sitting around tables with my oldest friends, family and people I have just met. A table is where we eat and talk, where we connect.

What and how we eat remains a source of constant fascination to me, as is how particular ingredients spread across the world. I want to make links and trace patterns. Food is about history, geography, our habits, imagination and how we relate to each other.

And there's still a lot to discover.

# I

# CRAZY WATER, PICKLED LEMONS

I came to live in London in my early twenties. I moved into a tiny basement flat, in the north of the city, which had a kitchenette with a cream carpet that was soon covered in stains. Everything had to be stored in one tall cupboard, which made it impossible to get at my saucepans without being attacked by an old upright Hoover. But any shortcomings were made up for by what I found around me.

At the end of my road there was a green-fronted Turkish grocery that, alongside loo rolls and tea bags, sold bottles of flower water, pails of flavoured olives and jars of sesame paste. A short trip to the Edgware Road led to the heart of London's Arab community, where, among the hookah pipes and mint tea drinking, I discovered sacks of pistachios and sour, shrivelled fruits called barberries. There were trays of Turkish delight, flavoured with lemon and orange blossom as well as rose water, and, in the autumn, I could come home from the local street market with bags of honeyed quince.

I bought Claudia Roden's *A New Book of Middle Eastern Food* and curled up with it on the sofa when I got home from work in the evenings. I may have been looking out at London rain, orange streetlights and the darkening feet of passers-by above me, but the writing – and the recipes – took me to Cairo. In my imagination, I went for afternoon tea with Roden's aunts in a place of tinkling glasses, tiny spoons and silver dishes of pure colour, where the fragrance of musk, ambergris and jasmine hung in the air. It was like an adult version of the *Arabian Nights*, except that now the treasure troves of jewels were bursting with ripe figs, sticky dates and glass phials of flower water. I was already a keen cook, but now, in my basement flat, a whole world opened up for me and it wasn't just one of new flavours. With this book, and these ingredients, I could travel while standing still.

As I cooked more, discovered new recipes and tried this or that restaurant, I realized there were particular foods and dishes I thought of as magical. There were ingredients whose properties were so unusual, or whose provenance so foreign, that they could, like the unicorn, have been invented by writers of myths: leathery pomegranates, their insides bursting with ruby seeds; saffron, the dried stigmas of crocus flowers gathered before dawn in Spanish fields. There were dishes that looked quite ordinary, but which had undergone such a transformation in cooking that I couldn't understand how they worked, such as Middle Eastern orange cake, made with unpeeled oranges, boiled, puréed, mixed with eggs, sugar and flour and baked to a citrusy moistness; or Persian ice cream, with its chewiness and rose-scented flavour, the product of flower water, powdered orchid root and ground mastic, an aromatic tree resin.

Then there were dishes whose poetry came from their evocative names or stories, as well as from their taste. Think of 'ice in heaven', a Middle Eastern milk pudding of rose-perfumed ground rice; or 'pearl diver's rice' – honey-sweetened rice from Bahrain to be eaten with lamb – so-called because its high sugar content was thought to help pearl divers stay under the water for longer; or 'crazy water', an Italian dish of sea bass poached in a salty, garlicky broth, cooked by the fishermen of the Amalfi coast. Other dishes just seemed magical to me by being out of the ordinary, bold in their simplicity or the apparent dissonance of their ingredients, such as Catalan stuffed chicken with honey and quince allioli.

Senses, as well as tastes, are locked up in food. The clear perfumed stillness of a bottle of flower water, the sexy, velvety skin of a fig, the sunburnt-blood colour of a jar of cayenne. Our love of foods has as much to do with what they represent as with what they taste like.

Nearly all the ingredients and dishes that, for me, have this other-worldly quality are from Spain, Portugal, the southern regions of France and Italy, the Middle East and North Africa. They are Mediterranean – or at least Southern European – dishes, but many of them are stamped with an Arab or Persian influence. This is aromatic, perfumed or sweet-and-sour food, food that is marked with the decorativeness of the culture from which it comes. Many of these dishes evolved when the Arabs took their love of fruits, nuts, spices, perfumes and sheer sensuality to the countries they conquered.

The ingredients I have found so exhilarating are now widely available, but this doesn't mean they have lost their charm. I love my forays to Middle Eastern shops, and the thrill of picking up foods in foreign markets, but I'm glad that I can get most of them without going too far. The specialness is in the food itself. It excites me to see a jar of pickled lemons wedged in between the ketchup and the cornflakes in my kitchen cupboard, a bottle of pomegranate molasses hiding behind the marmalade, or a scarlet-and-sky blue box covered with Arabic script nudged up against the bold English lettering on a bottle of HP sauce. It is a cupboard full of possibilities. It offers me the chance to experience the otherness of places by cooking and eating, to go on journeys with my tastebuds and my mind. With food, you don't have to buy an airline ticket or don a backpack; the magic of the unfamiliar is there, right beside the everyday, for you to bring into your kitchen.

# GARLIC AND LIQUID GOLD

When I was fifteen, I had a life-changing cookery lesson. At the kitchen table of a cottage in rural France, with Plastic Bertrand screaming 'Ça Plane Pour Moi' out of a tinny radio, I watched a master at work. My penpal Clothilde rubbed a cut clove of garlic around the inside of a china bowl. She then added Dijon mustard, wine vinegar, salt, pepper and a sprinkling of chopped chives. 'Always chives?' I asked. 'No, sometimes mint, sometimes parsley. *Ça dépend*. But always olive oil,' she said as she deftly added a stream of Provençal extra virgin, whisking all the time with a fork.

Green leaves of frisée lettuce were tossed into the bowl just before serving and we ate the salad after grilled pork chops marinated in olive oil, garlic and herbs served with potatoes fried in olive oil and garlic. What a lunch! Garlic had given it a bit of cheeky confidence; olive oil was its soul.

We did have olive oil back home, but it came in a Crosse & Blackwell bottle and was kept for medicinal purposes. Gently warmed, a teaspoonful of this healing syrup would be poured into aching ears. Returning from France, however, I demanded that olive oil be liberated from the medicine cabinet. I wanted it for cooking, marinating and dressing plain green leaves. There were to be no more vinaigrettes made with sunflower oil and shaken in a jam jar.

It took longer to get into the fruits of the olive tree. Jars of stuffed olives appeared in the fridge before my parents' parties. Little green olives with a flash of red pepper peeping out, they were indelibly marked as grown-ups' food. They whispered of martinis, Manhattan skylines and dates with men who played Frank Sinatra. But when I tasted them, bitter and briny, they made me shudder. Later, on holiday in Greece, olive trees themselves mesmerized me. Grey and gnarled, with shoals of silver fishes flickering at their fingertips, they were unknowable; constant yet ever-changing. And their rustle was everywhere. No wonder they confounded painters. Van Gogh told his brother that, 'The murmur of an olive grove has something very intimate, immensely old. It is too beautiful for me to try to conceive of it or dare to paint it.' And Renoir wrote: 'Look at the light on the olives. It sparkles like diamonds.

It is pink, it is blue, and the sky that plays across them is enough to drive you mad.'

When I tried moist purple and black olives on that holiday, they tasted salty and sweet, buttery and inky. They still made me shudder – they taste so aggressively of themselves – but now it was a thrill. A hunk of bread, sea salt, extra virgin olive oil and a scattering of these shiny bodies became one of my favourite meals. It tasted of an ancient world.

Shimmering among dry rocks and scrubland, olive trees *are* the Mediterranean – a constant reminder of the age of the area – and so sacred that, in parts of Greece, olive groves could only be tended by celibate men and virgins. Even today, one of the greatest insults a Greek can bestow on someone is to say that he or she is the kind of person who would cut down an olive tree. But you can only really understand why the olive is such a powerful symbol, and so central an ingredient, by steeping yourself in its flavours. Think of the simplest dishes: *aglio e olio* (pasta with sautéed garlic and warmed olive oil, and perhaps the addition of chilli or parsley), a dish so good you don't even want cheese on it; or the Catalan *pa amb oli* (literally 'bread and oil'), where oil is simply poured on toasted bread and seasoned with salt; or tapenade (black olives ground with olive oil and garlic to make a paste for bread, a dip for radishes or a kind of relish for grilled lamb and chicken). These are dishes in which food undergoes such minor treatment you could barely call it cooking, in which olives and their oil *are* the dish.

The fruit comes in many different shapes – reminiscent of torpedoes, chunky buttons or little beads – and even more flavours. Picked at various stages of maturity, their colours start at unripe sage green and travel through pinkish-grey, violet, purple and brown, to raven black. In markets from Marrakesh to Ménerbes, huge bowls of olives are perfumed with garlic, thyme or fennel, bathed in olive oil and harissa, or flecked with parsley, chilli and pickled lemons. It's easy to flavour your own: buy plain olives from a good delicatessen, wash them if they're in brine, then add extra virgin olive oil and flavourings. Give them a day and they'll be great; if you can leave them for a week, so much the better. Make slashes through to the stone if you want your aromatics to penetrate further.

Our appreciation of olives and olive oil has come a long way, perhaps too far, I recently thought, watching a chef in a reputed London restaurant pouring extra virgin over a plate of foie gras. It's fashionable to be fired up over single-estate Tuscans and organic Californians – they're the culinary equivalents of Prada handbags – but try to ignore the snobbery and just taste the stuff.

Like wine, the flavour of olive oil depends on the olive variety, soil, climate and the region in which the fruit is grown, as well as on how the oil is processed. The classification of the various grades of oil is strictly monitored. 'Extra virgin' is the richest oil, because it comes from the first pressing of the olives. To classify as extra virgin, the oil must not be adulterated in any way: the olives mustn't be treated, oil can be obtained only by pressing and no other oils can be added. Single-estate extra virgins, the *grands crus* of the oleaginous world, are, like wine, individual and vary in flavour from year to year. They're expensive and, like all olive oils, they don't keep well (store them in a cool place away from the light), so you can only really have one open at a time. But they are so varied that you never tire of using them and they transform the simplest of dishes: green beans, sliced tomatoes, baked fish, warm pulses, grilled chicken and fresh broths are all taken to wonderful heights with a distinctive olive oil and perhaps a squeeze of lemon juice. You can choose from the buttery, sweet flavour of an oil from Liguria, the fruitiness of one from Provence, or the grassy bitterness of a bottle of Tuscan.

A blended extra virgin is good for mustardy vinaigrettes and sauces such as pesto and salsa verde, where you want a good olive oil taste, but know that great subtlety would be lost against the other big flavours.

And you can't really talk about olive oil without, at the same time, thinking of garlic: the faint note it leaves if rubbed around the salad bowl; the sharpness it provides when grated against oil-drenched toast. Then there are the dishes in which oil and garlic magically combine to produce meals that are almost mystical, their history being so long and their invention so miraculous, such as aïoli. It's the garlic mayonnaise the Provençals call *le beurre de Provence* and is central to the feast *le grand aïoli*. Platters of hard-boiled eggs, raw summer vegetables and poached salt cod are served with big bowls of this rich yellow emulsion. Downed with bottles of Provençal rosé, *le grand aïoli* is like eating great punches of sunshine. And, to be honest, the aïoli is wonderful just with potatoes and none of the extra palaver. Try chips, aïoli and a bottle of Champagne for a fast, glitzy supper.

Then there's aïoli's Spanish cousin, the Catalan allioli ('garlic and oil'), a good-with-everything sauce that finds its way into paellas and pasta dishes and is *de rigueur* (or *cosa obligada*) with chicken, pork and lamb. In its truest form, allioli doesn't contain egg yolks, but is an amazing emulsification of crushed garlic cloves and oil. In practice, most Catalans do use egg yolk to stabilize it, because it is such a fragile concoction, and they also love tinkering with it. You might think that an allioli made with the addition of apples, pears or honey sounds revolting, but that is just the sort of culinary surprise a Catalan cook will spring on you.

These mayonnaises use crushed raw garlic, so you get it in its most aggressive form. The more garlic is cut, the more its chemicals are activated and the more pungent the flavour produced. Uncrushed, the flavour is much more subtle. Slice garlic and cook it long and slow in a braise and it will gently infuse the whole dish. Poach garlic in a little stock and cream, purée the cloves and add them back to the reduced cooking liquid and you have a gentle garlicky sauce for rare steak. Roast whole garlic bulbs until they're oozing caramel and squeeze the sweet flesh from each clove on to bread or grilled meats. New season's garlic – which hasn't yet had the chance to dry and has a mild flavour – arrives in the shops in June. It's moist and fleshy and is great roasted and served as a vegetable.

There are only two rules with garlic: never, ever burn it (it turns disgustingly bitter, though slivers of just-browned garlic are delicious) and don't use old stuff. If the head is crumbly or sprouting green shoots, chuck it out, because once garlic has seen better days it turns rancid and the smallest piece will ruin your dish.

I'm grateful for that afternoon with Clothilde. It was my first trip abroad and, amid the homesickness and problems with French boys (did they all taste of Roquefort when you kissed them?) I experienced a turning point in appreciating the good, but simple, things. Clo wouldn't have much truck with these Tuscan oils, (well, they're not French), but she'd certainly approve of the fact that I have long since abandoned the jam jar method for making vinaigrette, and that I always go through her soothing ritual of mixing it in the bottom of the salad bowl.

# 3
# *SOL O SOMBRA*

As soon as I get off the plane, I know I'm in Madrid. I might be walking through a calm, light-filled airport (the beautiful Madrid-Barajas), but I can feel the pull of somewhere darker. It starts first with the aroma – leather, garlic and cologne – then I hear the language. Smoking isn't as popular in Spain as it once was, but most of the men still sound as if they're on forty a day. The rich 'j' sounds – formed in the back of the throat – mean conversations are made up of woody growls as much as words. (VS Pritchett in *The Spanish Temper* referred to these as 'dry-throated gutturals', but that is only to hear the harshness and not the beauty.)

I first went to Spain to see a man about a horse. My dad was selling one – a show-jumper that had performed well at Dublin Horse Show – to a rider in Madrid. I had just sat O-level Spanish and was, ambitiously, going along as the translator. Speaking the language didn't bother me. But the bar where we met Luis was another matter. Spain is full of brightness – the sun, its flag, flamenco dresses – but also darkness. El Greco wasn't born in Spain, but he is a painter of Spain. Prints of his works hung on the wall outside my school Latin room. Full of dark figures who seemed to emanate light even though they were sombre and lugubrious, they formed my sense of the country. The literature we were studying in Spanish class was dark, too. Lorca's plays were all bitterness and repression. Machado, Spain's most famous poet, often wrote about the late afternoon, a time of shadows and melancholy. When we learned that Spaniards bought tickets for bull fights according to where they wanted to sit – *sol o sombra* – in sun or shade – it seemed entirely apt.

The bar in Madrid where we met Luis was an El Greco brought to life. Serious men lounged in old leather chairs; bottles of sherry, the colour of treacle and maple syrup, were lined up behind a green tiled bar. Voices were deep; smoke and a gorgeous smell of tobacco filled the air. I was the only female. A trip to France was my one previous experience of 'otherness' and this was much more foreign. It wasn't the Madrid of my Spanish grammar book, where Mercedes and Flores spent their afternoons boating in the Parque del Retiro. In our four days there, I found it a city of cavernous bars, magisterial buildings and terrible heat.

They say that in Madrid there are *nueve meses de invierno y tres meses de infierno* ('nine months of winter and three months of hell')... and the heat *was* infernal. I lay in bed every night and listened as they hosed the streets. Only when dawn broke was the city deemed to be clean of the previous day's dust and sweat.

The restaurants were as full of life as Machado was full of melancholy, dizzying in their noise level and energy. We sat at small tables where we were delivered plate after plate. I couldn't have dreamt up these dishes: a cold soup of almonds, bread, garlic and olive oil; fried squid with allioli and a gash of smoked paprika; every bit of a pig that you could name (and many that you couldn't); egg-rich pastries that seemed to be from another age. I loved the food. But by the time I left Madrid, I didn't know whether I felt the same about the country.

Foreigners have been accused of painting Spain as a dark place, as a *leyenda negra*, a 'black legend', full of cruel priests, inquisitors and grief. But I think this comes from Spanish paintings and literature. Lorca, after all, wrote, 'In Spain the dead are more alive than the dead of any other place.'

While studying A-level Spanish, the country's complexity became more understandable. We had a teaching assistant, Paz, from Salamanca. Franco had died in 1975 and Spain had moved, with seeming ease, to democracy. But in 1979 Paz would only talk about Franco in whispers, as if his ghost was hiding round the corners of this small Northern Irish school. She was scared of him. Democracy was only working because there was an unspoken understanding that everybody would push the Civil War, and the Franco years, away. It was a vow of silence, *el pacto del olvido*, 'the pact of forgetting'.

I think this Spain of two halves (and also of small states – the Basque country, Catalonia – that didn't want to belong to this larger entity) reminded me of my own country. Ireland had its darkness and light, too. The Troubles had been around for my entire childhood, and there'd been 'troubles' for years before that, so it was in many ways a grim place, but we, like the Spanish, were also good at enjoying ourselves and putting our best side to the world.

Paz held a small party for my Spanish class one night. We invited the other language assistants, lit a fire on the beach and ran crazily up and down the dunes, then cooked paella back at her flat (I'd had to look hard for langoustines and snails and, yes, the snails were canned). We danced until we all crashed out at about 4am. It was a high-octane night but, even so, Paz made sure there was a fissure of bleakness. She made us listen as she read from Ted Hughes's *Wodwo* – a collection full of feuds and destructiveness – before we fell asleep, as if we couldn't have a good time without also considering more serious things.

In the summer before I started university, I travelled round Spain, a country that still scared me, and I went *because* it scared me. Why would I have wanted the elegance of Italy, with its beautiful villas and rows of cypress trees, when I could have this difficult country instead? Ted Hughes later wrote, in *Birthday Letters*, about how Sylvia Plath hated Spain, how its 'oiled anchovy faces, the African black edges' had frightened her. I empathized, though that summer was also a summer of light. The Andalusian countryside was so white – scorched by heat – it hurt my eyes; Seville was a dream of hidden courtyards, orange trees, small white-washed squares, and intricately decorated tiles. I no longer saw Spain as an El Greco but as another painting I discovered in Madrid: *La tertulia del Café de Pombo*, by José Gutiérrez Solana. Spain was serious, yes, but it was a place I wanted to understand – and there was always wine and *jamón* on the table.

In contrast to the darkness, the bright side of Spain is about having a good time, about energy. Spaniards believe they have a right to enjoy themselves and they do so noisily and constantly. Food is part of this and so, too, is how Spaniards choose to consume it. Especially in Madrid, they defy normal sleeping hours. If they feel like it, they just ignore the night. You meet for dinner, but first you have to have tapas and drinks (in different locations). Dinner might not be eaten until 11pm, and then you party and then, finally, you go for churros. Eating and chatting can go on all night long. It's known as *trasnochar*, to 'stay up late', and it's mandatory to do this and still turn up for work looking bright-eyed.

I'm not going to stretch the darkness and light metaphor to fit the food, but *arroz negro*, 'black rice', which I first ate in Catalonia in my early twenties, was the most shocking and intense dish I had, at that time, ever tasted. Catalonia has the most surprising food in Spain. It balances elements and pushes them, too. There's the play of sweet with savoury. (It's the Moorish legacy, I love it most in allioli made with quince, apples or pears. A garlic mayonnaise made with fruit? Madness.) You also see dishes that combine food from the sea and the land (*mar i muntanya*), such as the classic chicken with prawns and pulverized chocolate, bread, nuts and herbs. It's not surprising that Catalonia gave birth to Ferran Adrià and molecular gastronomy (it produced Gaudí, after all, and is home to the Parc Natural del Cap de Creus, an area that influenced Salvador Dalí).

Adrià is about posing questions, pushing cooking to the limit, offering the unexpected. To try to capture and intensify the flavour of olives by dripping concentrated olive juice into calcium alginate to form a liquid sphere…

one of the only places this could have happened is Spain. Because Spain, despite its troubled past (or perhaps because of it, as people try to reach beyond the difficult and the shaming), is focused on the future. (You can see this in the country's architecture too: Richard Rogers has described Spain as 'Europe's architectural power house'.)

On the night I ate the black rice, I ended up in a little coastal town on the Costa Brava, the kind of pretty place artists go to paint, where a festival was in full swing. It was both strange and thrilling – locals were wearing frightening beaked masks and dancing in the street – and everyone was eating *buñuelos* (little deep-fried clouds of dough, lighter than doughnuts, dusted with sugar). My friend and I sat in a bar drinking *cremat*, a flaming mixture of dark rum, sugar, coffee, cinnamon and lemon peel. Set alight in a terracotta dish, the rum burns with the flavourings until only about two-thirds of the liquid remains, then it's ladled into cups of bitter coffee. It would be a daring way to end a meal, and a good way to contemplate darkness and light.

# 4

# PITH AND SKIN

When I was little, I used to get through a lot of an orange drink called Tree Top. The label featured a photograph of an orange tree: a network of dark, Christmas-green leaves, vivid little fiery globes and white blossom. I loved the picture; I used to sit on the floor and stare at it. But its beauty didn't seem to have anything to do with the oranges I ate, or, rather, didn't eat. In our house, we all fought over the portioning of strawberries, peaches and nectarines and even took an interest in the different varieties of apples that came and went, but bananas and oranges? Nah. There were always plenty of them; no need to get excited.

Then, on a school trip to Mallorca, we went on a rickety train – all rattling wooden carriages and no windowpanes – from Palma to Sóller. The route cut through the centre of the island, and, quite unexpectedly, my breath was taken away by the view through the window. We were in the middle of orange groves, acres of them; I could almost put my hand out of the window and touch them. They were so beautiful that they didn't seem real. 'Surely these are trees for dolls,' I thought. Both leaves and oranges looked like they had been carved from wood, stained and polished. Suddenly the orange assumed all the romanticism of the mango. Soon after this, I began to fancy myself as the girl in the Leonard Cohen song who sipped her tea with oranges 'that came all the way from China' (which is where they did originally come from), and began to taste and appreciate those fluorescent mounds that sat on the greengrocers' shelves.

I have loved oranges ever since, especially as they are at their best just when you need them: in the middle of winter. Whoever was responsible for designing nature, this was one of their more inspired touches.

It was the bitter, or Seville, orange (the one still used for making marmalade) that arrived in the Mediterranean first. Like so many foods, it was brought there by the Arabs. In fact, the path the Arabs took – as they swept their way across to North Africa and up into Spain and Sicily – is marked in citrus groves. The Arabs planted glowing terraces of orange trees in Sicily and squares of them against the whitewashed walls of Sevillian courtyards. Orange trees had the power to enchant.

French kings started building orangeries and importing the trees from Italy, bathing the roots in milk and honey before planting them in pots with wheels. These would be wheeled outside so that the trees, like foreign royalty, could enjoy the warmth of sunny days, returning to their glasshouse when the coolness of late afternoon descended. The Medici incorporated oranges into their coat of arms, while Renaissance painters, quite inaccurately, started sticking orange trees behind Christ and the Virgin Mary. For a long time it was oranges-a-go-go, the fruits admired as much for their beauty and fragrance as for their taste.

The orange's popularity as a food really took off when the sweet version arrived on the scene, grown first by the Portuguese. But it's in the countries where oranges were planted that you still find the most interesting orange dishes. Sicilians mix the zest and juice with nuts and raisins and use it to stuff sardines, and they serve grilled tuna with a sweet-sour orange sauce. Andalusians cook duck with green olives and oranges and will offer you a wedge to squeeze over a veal chop. Moroccans sprinkle sliced sweet oranges with flower water and cinnamon for the easiest dessert in the world. Both the Italians and the Spanish make wonderful salads with oranges, putting the sweetest specimens against inky black olives, cleansing fennel, woody sherry vinegar and even raw salt cod. For a truly grown-up appreciation of the orange, just slice some good navel oranges, layer them with wafer-thin red onions and anoint the whole thing with extra virgin olive oil. It might sound like summer eating, but these salads bring great shocks of sunshine to wintering tastebuds.

It isn't always easy to find good oranges, as appearance is no indication of flavour. A perfectly formed glowing little orb can taste pallid. A pale, misshapen, pockmarked orange can be delicious. Valencia oranges have a smooth, thin skin and are juicy, but navels – they're the ones with a 'belly button' in one end – have the best flavour. They're definitely 'the only fruit': mouth-puckeringly citrusy, easy to peel and almost seedless. And the Sicilian raspberry-hued blood orange, that once-a-year treat? Don't get me started: scarlet, sweet, sharp, stunning. May they always be an occasional joy. The most sensible thing to do is buy a couple of oranges at a time from the greengrocer and, if they're good, go back the next day and buy a big bag of the same batch. The navels I bought this winter were so good that, some nights, I didn't even cook; I just set a bag of navel oranges on the sofa and ate them in front of the telly.

I'm not one for fancy orange desserts. Let this fruit be itself. I simply want slices or segments bathed in light citrus syrups flavoured with lime and cardamom, orange flower water, mint, rosemary, even tarragon. They're also good in the kind of spicy red wine syrup in which you usually poach pears. And don't let anyone tell you that oranges in caramel is an abomination of the 1970s. Done well (I mean with tasty oranges and a syrup that isn't burnt) it's a great dish; made with blood oranges it's spectacular. These oranges-in-syrup dishes are good with oranges alone, but some of them are even better with the additional colours and flavours that grapefruits, blood oranges and pomelos bring. It's lovely to see the various shades floating in a bowl together.

Sorbets and granitas are two of the best ways to get a mouthful of pure citrus essence. Grapefruit with mint produces a sorbet that looks – and refreshes – like a glassful of snow; blood orange mixed with pomegranate juice and vodka makes a stunning granita of garnet shards and glassy seeds; orange and mandarin are great on their own.

Cakes give you the chance to take advantage of the orange's perfume rather than its zing. The perfume is in the zest – you can see sprays of the oil when you peel an orange – and that's what a cake needs. You can kid yourself by adding more juice in place of zest, but you won't get away with it. And if you're going to use the zest, buy unwaxed organic oranges. I know they say you can scrub the wax off, but starting a recipe with a brush and washing-up liquid is not my idea of a good time (and that goes for lemons, too).

Ah, lemons too... They could never be an 'also ran', neither in the culinary nor the visual stakes. One early Arab poet described the oranges of Sicily as 'blazing fire among the emerald boughs,' while the lemons, in comparison, wore 'the paleness of a lover who has spent the night crying...' It's doubtful whether even lack of love could diminish the lemon, though. I'm fond of the odd big dipper ride for my tastebuds, such as, Mexican-style, sucking a bit of salted lemon or lime and then throwing a shot of tequila down my throat. My three-year-old likes the same kind of shock, as he puckers and grimaces in delight, chewing on a lemon slice stolen from a jug of lemonade. Sicilians, mind you, will slice a piece of fresh lemon, salt it and chew it without so much as a quiver.

It's good to remind yourself of the power of lemon: so much more than just a fruit, but a seasoning as potent as salt or sugar, a flavour-heightener *par excellence*. When something seems to be missing from a dish, the hidden element can often be found in a lemon. It works in mysterious ways, making the parsley in a parsley sauce taste greener, mangoes taste sweeter and rose water more floral and less cloying. Lemon makes nearly everything taste more of itself. Fish is nothing without lemon – it brings out the sweetness and restores the taste of the sea – but try it squeezed over steak and grilled lamb, too.

Lemon's sharp juice also sours and tenderizes. Few dishes in the Middle Eastern kitchen escape this fruit – marinating cubes of lamb, high-octane salads of parsley and onion, purées of chickpeas and aubergines all bear its stamp – and North African cooks even treat lemons whole, subduing their astringency by draining out some of their acidity with salt.

Once preserved, the brightness of lemons turns a mellow, translucent gold. Their flavour is salty and slightly sour, but they have none of the rasping acidity of the fresh fruit. Make a jar and you'll soon be addicted to the taste, employing them not just in Moroccan tajines, but in a dish of Mediterranean vegetables, with olive oil-roast potatoes and red onions, in bowls of bulgur wheat, couscous and pulses. Or try their preserved peel, in place of grated fresh lemon zest, with finely chopped parsley and garlic for a twist on an Italian gremolata that makes a deeper, richer addition to meaty, tomatoey stews. In Egypt, a bowl of preserved lemons is often served with mezze, so each diner can take quarters to eat with pulses, particularly the bean dish *ful medames*.

Pickling lemon slices is another way to preserve and soften the fruit's character. Salt cut lemons overnight, then layer them in a jar with stripes of paprika and bathe them in olive oil. They will glow on the shelves of your cupboard, suggesting possibilities the other jars never could.

I often use these as I would preserved lemons, remembering that the paprika gives them an additional kick: chop them up with black olives and parsley for a salad, or add them to a braise of chicken or lamb. Lay whole slices on fish fillets and bake in the oven, or tuck them into a pan full of chicken joints and wedges of red onion for roasting. And don't forget the lemon-infused oil: it's brilliant for vinaigrettes.

Oranges provide a culinary wake-up call; lemons are indispensable. And even if you're not in the mood for cooking, it's still worth giving in to the impulse to buy those big string bags of citrus colour. Just pile the oranges in a bowl, the lemons in another and put them somewhere prominent. The beauty of some foods is as important as the taste.

5

# THE SPICE TRAIL

Spices embody our love of the romantic. Stored in little packets, glass jars, boxes or tins, every ingredient is rendered special. They are small postcards from the edges of the world, synonymous with the east and the Arabian peninsula even when, as with cumin and coriander, their provenance is actually the Mediterranean. Empires have been built on the back of them, wars waged over them and world-altering explorations undertaken to find them. They have always enchanted.

Two of the most alluring spices are saffron and cardamom: cardamom because its flavour is so elusive – the dishes it flavours feel as if a ghost has walked through them – saffron for those blood-red threads that turn whole platters of food into gold, bleeding yolk-yellow streaks over creamy chicken and milky white yogurt. It seems extraordinary that anyone thought of cooking with the stigmas of a flower, the crocus, but nearly everything about saffron is other-worldly: that the stigmas have to be picked from mauve-ribboned fields early in the morning, before sun, rain or wind can damage them; that the blossoms, separated from the red stigmas, turn the pickers' hands blue with their juice; that women with decades of experience dry the stigmas over heat using no gauge other than their nose and eyes. Yet saffron must be used sparingly, as it has an inherent bitterness and a pungency of mushrooms. It has to perfume food rather than suffuse it; a good job, since it is by far the most expensive spice. The Persians, with their love of jewelled food, adore saffron and colour handfuls of rice saffron-yellow before scattering them over dishes of white rice grains. In Moroccan and Spanish cooking, saffron haunts tomato sauces and tomato-based fish soups, giving a subtle, smoky spiciness.

Saffron seems at its most extravagant in desserts – you feel like you're cooking with gold – but here you must be very restrained, or its flavour will jar. Try just a tad in a delicate ice cream, a smidgen in a pistachio-studded rice pudding, a few threads in a pan of honey-poached apricots.

Cardamom needs a light touch too. Cardamom seeds, when released from their pods and ground, smell of roses and liquorice. When I'm cooking with cardamom, I visualize it as a misty vapour wafting through food. (Cleopatra actually did turn cardamom to smoke, burning it in her chambers during Mark Antony's visits.) I always want its flavour to be stronger and yet, if it is, the effect is destroyed. An excess of cardamom tastes of the chemist's shop. Cardamom's a flavour best yearned for. Add it in whispers.

Cardamom's perfume easily infuses cream; use it in rice pudding, white or dark chocolate mousse and to make heavenly ice cream. Try it in citrus syrups too: make one with orange juice, honey and cardamom for bathing orange slices, or even just for drizzling on ice cream or milky puddings. Coffee is another good partner, hardly surprising when you think that half of the cardamom produced in the world ends up in Arabic coffee. The spice is usually ground into the drink, but the Bedouin tribes of North Africa place cracked pods in the spout of the coffee pot itself. A few ground pods added to coffee cake or coffee ice cream subtly changes their whole character.

In the same way that saffron's magic is increased when added to sweet dishes, cinnamon's allure is enhanced when added to savoury food. Cinnamon, along with allspice, is the spice for those little meatballs of minced lamb – kofta – you find all over the Middle East. Cinnamon really brings out the sweetness of lamb. I put a pinch in my otherwise very British shepherd's pie and make a lovely savoury-sweet Greek-inspired dish of minced lamb with chopped dates and cinnamon encased in filo.

When it comes to puddings, I could live without cinnamon, though I like the Moroccan habit of sprinkling it on flower water-perfumed oranges. Cinnamon's effect on sweetness is cloying, its image too cute. I'd rather have sassy ginger, the Lucille Ball of the spice world, pepping up my sugar rushes. Plucky, assertive and, when fresh, full of tongue-prickling juice, ginger – with its tight beige skin, veined like slub silk – comes in many forms: there's fresh root ginger (not a root at all but a rhizome, or underground stem, of the plant); ground powder; slices pickled in vinegar or tender nuggets in syrup. Preserved, ginger's a great store cupboard standby for chopping up and mixing into creamy rhubarb, plum or apple fools. Make ginger syrup by simmering slices of fresh ginger in a sugar syrup until the required piquancy is reached. Enhance the syrup's fragrance with fresh lime, star anise or chopped lemongrass and you have a fragrant sauce for sliced mango or melon. Ginger syrup is a good medium in which to poach apricots, too, or knead a little of the powdered spice into nuggets of marzipan to stuff pears or plums for baking.

In savoury dishes we associate ginger with Chinese, Thai and Indian food. But Moroccans love it too; they always use it in the powdered form, which is hotter and more warming, without the tangy freshness of the root. Ginger goes into rich tajines of meat and fruit where, alongside saffron, cinnamon, cumin and cayenne, it mellows to a warm sweet glow. Moroccans use ginger with fish too, especially shad, which is rubbed with ginger and filled with ginger-and-rice-stuffed dates.

Chillies are a minefield and not just for your tastebuds. They come in so many forms and strengths: fresh, dried, powdered and flaked; from long tapering green fingers, just mild enough to pickle for the mezze table, to the lethal tiny red tongues of fire called bird's eyes. There are several hundred varieties, all part of the great capsicum family.

Cayenne pepper is usually ground from a single variety and is hot, about seven on a scale of one to ten; paprika, which developed in Hungary after the Turks took chillies there, and the Spanish *pimentón*, are ground from several chillies and come in both hot and sweet forms. Cayenne and paprika are used throughout the Middle East, though more for their underlying fruitiness than for heat. For burn, Algerians and Tunisians make the biting red chilli paste called harissa, a must for adding to couscous broth.

*Pimentón* is Spanish paprika and comes in two forms. *Pimentón de la Vera* is smoked and has a sweet, woody, smoked bacon flavour; it's great added to mayonnaise to be eaten with seafood, mixed with olive oil and lemon to make a marinade for chicken, or sprinkled on olive oil-roast potato wedges. Regular *pimentón* is sundried and not that different from Hungarian paprika.

I always keep a jar of chilli flakes handy. Once they're heated in a little olive oil, they give any dish a shot in the arm. When there's not much food in the fridge, sauté a few sliced garlic cloves, add a sprinkling of chilli flakes, a bunch of finely chopped parsley, a squeeze of lemon juice and some salt, toss with warm spaghetti and you have a great heat-speckled supper.

Cumin has none of the beauty of chillies, nor the intrigue of ginger, but it's my favourite spice. A real workhorse, its coarse, ridged seeds smell of earth and life: fresh sweat, dust, maleness. Walk through an Arab market anywhere and cumin, mingled with orange flower water, fresh coriander and mint, is the underlying odour. It seems to come from peoples' skin, as well as the stalls. Cumin's earthiness goes well with the most basic of ingredients: fried potatoes and pulses. It can provide a supporting bass note above which more shrill spices sing, but it more often dominates. In Morocco it's used as a kind of pepper; little dishes of salt and ground cumin are offered with grilled chicken and lamb, or hard-boiled eggs. In Egypt you can buy a street snack of eggs with little paper cones of dukka – a mixture of salt, pepper, roughly ground toasted cumin, coriander and sesame seeds and perhaps also hazelnuts – in which to dip them. Try quail's eggs with dukka. Or mix butter with crushed garlic, cayenne and freshly ground cumin to make a spice paste for the Moroccan lamb dish, *mechoui*. In Morocco they cook huge sides of spiced lamb on a spit; at home get a big shoulder of lamb, make incisions all over it and rub the spiced butter into gashes in the meat. Cook long and slow in the oven until meltingly tender and serve with flatbread, lemon wedges and little bowls of salt and cumin.

In Europe, only the Spanish and Portuguese use cumin – and sparingly at that – but they do great things with it. Try marinating chicken joints in honey, cumin, garlic and lemon before roasting them for a good sour-sweet bolt of Catalonia, or fry waxy sliced potatoes with a mixture of cumin and smoky *pimentón*.

Coriander seeds, with their echoes of orange zest and toasted hazelnuts, complement cumin. I love the sound of freshly toasted coriander and cumin seeds – and they should be toasted and freshly ground as their oils are volatile – cracking and splintering as you pound them.

The only rules with spices are to buy them in small quantities, so you don't harbour tasteless jars of old powder, and to grind freshly the ones which most benefit from it.

# 6
# AROUND THE TABLE

I'm ticking off the items on my list, scribbled, as usual, on the back of an envelope. The pears are lying in the pool of Marsala in which they've baked, and a glossy rubble of warm lentils with sausages on top has just come out of the oven. The table looks good. I've spent a lifetime collecting battered old cutlery and soft tablecloths and I love setting the table, even though I never do anything formal. There's just time to stick on a bit of lipstick – I rarely manage to change – before friends arrive. I feel a small thrill of excitement, but it's about the event rather than the food. Things happen at the table.

A meal is always about more than the dishes served. Food isn't just physical sustenance, it's also about pleasure and about people. The table is just as important as the oven or the hob. Having friends over is a performance of sorts.

Casualness is now *de rigueur*, but even casualness requires a bit of thought. Despite what I do for a living, I don't often have big crowds of people round to eat. I tend to cook for friends who are staying, or small groups.

I do uphold the kitchen table's role in our lives on a daily basis, though, which is a challenge when your children are teenagers. I won't relinquish our meals together and I know that if I let them slide for a few days we are all less happy. Sitting at the table is where we look at each other; the table makes it impossible not to. Then we talk, and if the food is good, we're happy. We also, it's true, argue. But we communicate and, in a time when everything can be texted or emailed or sent on WhatsApp, that's important.

The table is under threat. We eat alone more, on the sofa, standing up in the kitchen, at our computers, on the go. We try to squash eating into busy lives. Not all cultures sit round a table to eat (estimates suggest that about one-quarter of the world's population eat around a mat) and we haven't always done it in the west either. I'm not going to pretend that meals taken at a table are always and everywhere happy. They've served as a very conservative force (think of that Norman Rockwell Thanksgiving painting where everyone is relentlessly smiling). The 1950s American educational film *A Date with Your Family* – you can watch it online – now looks shocking in its emphasis on the roles assigned for the evening meal. The mother and daughter change their clothes because, the narrator tells us, 'The women of this family seem to feel that they owe it to the men of the family to look relaxed, rested and attractive,' later adding, 'The table is no place for discontent.'

It is, in fact, often a place of discontent. Many of the most memorable scenes in movies are about relationships collapsing at the table; in the Danish film, *Festen,* an entire extended family implodes, and in *American Beauty* the marriage between Lester and Carolyn Burnham bites the dust as the combatants fight across a table. A platter of asparagus ends up being thrown at the wall, the etiquette of the table literally smashed.

If there are fault lines – in friendships, in marriages, in a family – the table is where they will be most evident.

But the table is, generally, a place where good things happen, or at least we hope they will. In 18th-century Dutch, a good friend is called a 'table friend'. When food is scarce – I'm particularly thinking of the meals that Russians put together when the country was part of the Soviet Union and it was hard to get hold of much – people try to create a feast that can be served at the table, even if it's just *salade Olivier* made with tinned vegetables and industrial mayonnaise, pickled cabbage, buckwheat and vodka.

In the last eighteen months, I've had more large groups of people over to eat than I've had in years, and have been strongly reminded of what magical things can happen over a table. The American writer Adam Gopnik has said, 'The test of a meal is the talk that it makes.' It's better if the food is good, of course – if you're bothering to have people over you want them to experience pleasure, that is your gift to them – but it can be good in an ordinary way. Things have changed. As a child in the 1970s, I used to pore over the cookery pages in my mum's magazines, mentally noting what I would eventually need to pull off a bit of entertaining when I grew up (basically a chignon and a hostess trolley). Then, in the 1980s – when I started cooking for friends in earnest – I served up ridiculously complicated nouvelle cuisine meals that took days to prepare. But once molecular gastronomy came along, we all stopped trying to be chefs in our homes (thank God), because none of us had the kit.

After a particular lovely lunch one Sunday, my eldest child simply said: 'Let's do this more.' We'd invited old neighbours – a big sprawling garrulous family – and disparate friends who had just moved to London. People got to know each other simply by passing salt and bread, chairs were rearranged as small groups formed, noise levels were high, many jokes had been told, and I hadn't even bothered to serve the pudding 'nicely' (I brought the ice cream to go with the baked fruit to the table in its plastic tub). The food had been good, but not difficult or spectacular; everything had been transformed by the heat of the oven. As I looked at the mess when everyone had gone, words formed in my head, words that rang even truer than Gopnik's: 'Your reward for cooking is laughter,' I thought.

# 7
# CRAVING SALT

You know those late-night cravings you get? Those that compel some people to consider trading their granny for a tub of Ben & Jerry's ice cream or a bag of hot vinegary chips? Well, my cravings can be sated by slivers of rosy-pink flesh eaten straight from the can, olive oil dripping inelegantly down my chin. My fix? Anchovy fillets. They provide a bolt of such intense salty fishiness that my tastebuds, previously in a frenzy of expectation, are calmed and satisfied. I may look like a Spanish fisherman, but I sigh contentedly and go back to watching the late-night movie.

Salted anchovies and salt cod are synonymous with the Mediterranean, conjuring up visions of blue-and-red-painted boats, fishermen emptying throngs of glinting fish on to the harbour and black-clad old ladies tending terracotta pans, the pungent smell of their contents drifting up towards a statuette of the Blessed Virgin perched over the stove. Salt cod is almost a religious icon. It's the *fiel amigo* or 'faithful friend' of the Portuguese, while in Spain a person of importance is known as *el que corta el bacalao* or 'he who cuts the salt cod'.

Cod has sustained the Christian Mediterranean through centuries of Lent fasts, but the fish doesn't come from the region; it has always been caught in the Atlantic and North Sea by the British, Irish, French, Scandinavians, Portuguese and Basques. The Basques were catching – and salting – cod in the waters near Newfoundland before the Americas had been 'discovered', but, as they valued fish over land, they kept quiet about where it came from.

Outside the Mediterranean and West Indies, salt cod is harder to sell. It has the grey-white colour of over-washed underwear, looks like part of a corset and smells like old socks. And anyway, who wants to eat salty fish? The thing is, if salt cod has been properly soaked, it shouldn't be unpalatably salty. Its character will be different from that of regular cod – its flavour distilled, its fishiness deepened – but it tastes less salty than anchovies.

The American food writer Colman Andrews has written, in his book *Catalan Cuisine*, that the difference between salt cod and fresh cod is akin to that between fresh pork and cured pork: salt cod is a kind of bacon of the sea. Soak salt cod for two days, changing the water three times each day, then taste a bit: the fish should only be slightly salty. After that, it's easy to use. It's often served as salt cod fritters, or in a rough purée. The French make *brandade de morue*, blending poached salt cod, garlic, warm olive oil, milk and sometimes a little potato. Italians have their own version of this, *baccalà mantecato*, which is made in much the same way. Pile spoonfuls on to toasted croûtes and drizzle with olive oil for a starter or with an apéritif. You can even eat salt cod raw, once it's been soaked. Catalans eat thumb-thick shreds in a salad with tomatoes, olives and pepper strips. But my favourite raw treatment is paper-thin slices, moistened with strong extra virgin olive oil and lemon juice, topped with finely chopped garlic and parsley. For this, and any dish in which you want large pieces of fish, buy salt cod taken from the middle, the thickest, meatiest part. In Portuguese shops, you'll find a dozen grades; elsewhere you'll have the choice of the middle or the more gelatinous tail-end bits, which are fine for puréeing.

Fresh anchovies are so beautiful – shimmering slivers of quicksilver – that it seems a shame not to eat them as they are. But once they're beheaded, gutted and layered with salt crystals, they're even better. Their mild white flesh turns pale pink and develops a rich, deep flavour, both fishy and meaty at the same time. You see them packed into glass jars or round cans in which their salt-encrusted bodies lie arranged like the spokes of a wheel. Just wash the fish gently, pull away the backbones and pat them dry. Use them as they are, or cover them with olive oil and keep them in the fridge for up to two weeks.

Most food writers tell you to buy these salted anchovies, but I actually prefer anchovies packed in olive oil, as long as they are of really good quality. These have already gone through the salting process, but someone else has taken the trouble to rinse and fillet them before slipping them into their olive oil bath. The oil softens the salt, the anchovies flavour the oil and they both have a wonderful unctuous limpidity. Anchovies and olive oil were made for each other. Packed in cans, anchovies become one of the greatest convenience foods invented. Just peel back the lid and there, with a thick slice of country bread and a few tomatoes, is your lunch. Or try something a little more complicated: chop the fillets and add them to a vinaigrette with parsley and crushed garlic to pour over sliced tomatoes, warm waxy potatoes or slivers of roast red pepper, or mash half a dozen fillets with softened butter and rosemary, or a scoopful of crushed black olives, for a savoury butter to melt over beef or lamb steaks.

Despite their strong identity, anchovies enhance other flavours. They make you appreciate the mild: try eating halved hard-boiled eggs with spoonfuls of puréed anchovy. They dance enticingly with the sweet: mix them with slow-cooked onions, peppers and tomatoes. And they meld with and deepen the meaty: stuff anchovy halves along with slivers of garlic into a leg of lamb and you'll see what I mean.

Bottarga, the semi-dried and salted roe of grey mullet or tuna, sold in a moulded sausage shape, is a luxury that is eaten in Turkey, Egypt, France and Italy. It's the coral-brown colour of the darker patches of smoked salmon and is served in fine curling slices that have a dense, almost waxy texture. Like anchovies, bottarga has an intense salty-fishy quality which is perfect against mild flavours – try it with pasta and bread – and delicate salad leaves. It doesn't need to be cooked; in fact, don't do anything to it. It could become addictive, especially if, like me, you get late-night salt cravings...

# 8

# HARDY HERBS

I am not, by choice, an early riser. My sons joke that the only thing that gets me out of bed willingly is the scent of fresh coffee and hot croissants. But it's different when I'm on holiday in Provence. There, as soon as it starts getting light, you can find me with my nose stuck out of the bedroom window. I might go back to bed afterwards, but it's worth disturbing even the deepest of sleeps to take in that 6am scent of grass and herbs as they begin to grow warm. Of all the smells in the world – wild strawberries, bacon sarnies, the sweet bready scent of a baby's head – this is my favourite. A mixture of savory, lavender, wild thyme and rosemary, the aroma could not be described as 'sweet'. This is the *garrigue*, a sun-baked scrubland of poor soil, harsh light and olive trees. The scent is pungent: pine needles, pepper, camphor and citrus. I like it best in the morning because it's softer, promising hot weather and herb-marinated chops for lunch. By midday, when every footfall releases its scent and your head is pulsing in time with the cicadas, you'll be almost drunk with it and half asleep (not just a fanciful notion; oil of lavender is a relaxant, so it isn't only the heat that makes you drowsy).

With hardy herbs, we are firmly in Europe, land of rosemary-stuffed lamb and oregano-topped pizzas. But that doesn't mean they're dull. These feisty little plants have the potential to deliver dishes every bit as unusual as those from Africa and the Middle East. You do have to look at them afresh, though. Take rosemary, for example. For years, I've been throwing it on to focaccia, or into the roasting tin with chicken, garlic and potatoes. A meaty fish such as monkfish can stand up to it and I love to use the stalks as a natural skewer for scallops or chunks of lamb. When rosemary is abundant – and great bushes of it seem to lurk round every suburban corner – it's a treat thrown on to the coals of a barbecue or even, in winter, on to the fire.

Like the Italians, I love rosemary and use it a lot; what more could I want of it? Then I came across a chocolatier in Provence, Joël Durand in Saint-Rémy, who uses rosemary to flavour dark chocolate; a weird combination, you might think, but it works. This led me to try rosemary with other sweet things and I found its pine-scented herbiness was wonderful in all sorts of wintry puddings. Put a sprig in the poaching liquid for pears or plums; scatter rosemary's leaves over an upside-down apple cake; infuse the herb in a custard to make an ice cream for any of these fruits, or in cider for a syllabub, or – my favourite of all – in a citrus syrup for a winter salad of blood oranges, navel oranges and ruby-red grapefruit. I get a real thrill out of seeing a rosemary sprig floating, unexpectedly, in this bowl of glowing slices.

The Med may be rosemary's home, but this herb will survive the chill of a colder climate and even the worst gardener can't kill it. It's always there at the back door, its sprigs standing like miniature pine trees. Value its steadfastness and take advantage of it.

Rosemary can be a bit of a brute; too much of it and your dish will taste of the pharmacy (Elizabeth David rather tartly commented that there was no place for it in her kitchen except in a vase), but with a light hand, this herb can grace much more than the odd leg of lamb.

I'm not going to suggest that you put oregano in your puddings, but it's still worth getting to know it better. Oregano is the wild herb from which the milder marjoram was bred and it's the one most likely to be left for years on the shelves of a spice rack, turning to dust in its jar, misunderstood and underrated. I would throw the odd bit of oregano into tomato sauce or on to a pizza (it's the classic herb for both), but I didn't really appreciate it until

I bought some Greek oregano, or *rigani* as it's called there. A stronger, sharper version of Italian oregano, the Greek stuff is rich, resinous and peppery, permeating to the core of whatever it coats and able to withstand chillies, olives, capers, anchovies and the rigours of flames and long, slow cooking.

*Rigani* means 'joy of the mountains' and cushions of it soften hillsides all over Greece. Dried and sold in fuzzy green bunches, *rigani* is rubbed into meaty fish, roasts and kebabs, added to pots of bubbling tomatoes and aubergines and ground into meatballs and soups. It's the bossiest herb in the garden. The great thing is that it's actually better dried than fresh; drying concentrates its flavour rather than subduing it. I keep a big bunch of dried *rigani* in a tall jar and, on evenings when the supermarket has sold out of every other fresh herb, I can still have a Mediterranean grilling fest.

Sicilians make *salmoriglio* with fresh oregano, mixing the leaves with extra virgin olive oil, lemon juice, salt and pepper to create a vibrant sauce for tuna, swordfish and lamb. In other Southern Italian regions, oregano joins chilli in marinades for chops or chicken, a knockout combination. But remember that any oregano grown away from a burning hot climate, whether it's fresh or dried, will be much milder in flavour, so taste it before using it.

The strength of thyme is also affected by where it's grown. The bunch of wild stuff you buy in a Provençal market, already dried by the sun's glare, is a long way from the thyme in your Northern European garden, but both are fragrant with the thymol which gives the herb its distinctive flavour.

Thyme isn't the bully that oregano and even rosemary can be, yet it mixes well with both. It can simultaneously imprint its own special flavour and meld well with other ingredients. It can be soft and sweet in a soup of creamy carrots, or tap-dance on grilled prawns, and it's the only one of these hardier herbs that is gentle enough to work with eggs and cheese. I like it for this: that its fragile twiggy little body has such pluck, and, at the same time, such generosity.

In the past, I've nearly always used thyme with other herbs, but lately I've been letting it be its own sweet self. Its oils are volatile when heated, so a final scattering of fresh leaves into a dish of braised lamb or grilled chicken just heightens its fragrance.

As far as puddings go, I'd try thyme with anything I'd put rosemary in, as well as with more eggy puds: baked custards or the French batter pudding, clafoutis, for example. Thyme's also good in some preserves, such as apple jelly and orange marmalade, while its soft leaves are easily incorporated into bread doughs and cake batters.

There are hundreds of varieties of thyme, so you can mess around with the citrus varieties, lemon and orange (good for cakes), or aniseedy caraway thyme (try this in bread dough).

I have always associated the fragrance of lavender with my grandmother. On her bathroom windowsill, she kept a big bottle of lavender water, using it as both a skin toner and bath scent. Since she had soft, peachy cheeks right into her eighties, it must have worked. (She wasn't alone in this habit, of course; countless other grannies use lavender water and the ancient Romans added lavender sprigs to their bath water. Indeed, the name 'lavender' actually comes from the Latin *lavare*, 'to wash'.) The image of lavender growing in great purple swathes across the Provençal countryside is firmly stamped over this, making the herb seem less twee: less reminiscent of bags of pot pourri and more like hot, sweaty afternoons.

Adding fragrance, a breath of Provence and purpleness to food just seemed irresistible. I started to imagine lavender with freshly ground almonds, in cakes or the frangipane of a tart. I tried it in the poaching liquid for apricots, peaches and cherries, added it to shortbread and clafoutis. The faintest hint of lavender can be achieved by making lavender sugar, blending the flowers and granulated sugar together in a coffee grinder or food processor until you have a floral icing sugar. Showers of this can be sifted over fruit-topped meringues or stirred into delicate set custards and mousses, adding a flavour which diners can't quite identify. Lavender and honey ice cream gives the most intense 'essence-of-lavender' result; eating pale gold scoops of it with raspberries, you can almost hear the midday buzzing of bees, and friends react as if you've cooked with a magic potion: 'Lavender ice cream, oh my God!'

Savoury dishes don't have to miss out either. Lavender actually tastes like a mild version of rosemary with a breath of the floral wreathed around it. I love a lavender, honey and balsamic marinade for duck or chicken – it always amazes me that those delicate little purple flowers can take on such meaty partners – while a plum and lavender sauce, or a savoury apple and lavender jelly, is a great partner to pork. Unfortunately, lavender hasn't yet appeared in the herb section of our supermarkets, so you need to grow it, or beg or steal it from a gardener. Obviously it shouldn't be sprayed with anything and try and harvest it when the buds are out but not fully open: that's when the flavour is at its most powerful. You can sometimes find dried lavender in the shops, but make sure it can be used for cooking, rather than throwing in the bath, and replace fresh lavender in recipes with half the amount of dried.

We tend to think much more about basic ingredients – a good chicken, a fresh fish – than the additions. But just as you might deliberate over a plain string of pearls, a pair of gaudy glass earrings or a fine silver chain to go with that little black dress, think about how herbs can create a totally different mood and tone. They are the invaluable accessories of the culinary world, both for everyday wear or for dressing up.

# 9

# FALLING IN LOVE WITH FRANCE

Dark, flat sheets of cloud hung in the sky above me. By the time I got to Daniel's they belched rain, and I could hear the snarl of thunder. Daniel lived in a poor bit of Bordeaux, in an old apartment with his family, an angry father who swore through every meal, his bird-like grandma, with her floral housecoats and heavily pencilled eyebrows, and his large, silent grandpa who never said anything, except to ask for the salt. I was working as an au pair at a small family-run zoo outside Bordeaux. Daniel was my boyfriend and the zoo-keeper. I often had supper at his place.

On this stormy day, the film star Romy Schneider had died. Grandma was in tears. In honour of Romy, a bit more money than usual had been spent, there was *oeufs mayo* and leeks vinaigrette, a hunk of beef, pot-roasted with tomatoes and carrots and cut into soft slices, salad and Roquefort.

The bathroom in that apartment was housed in a few sheets of corrugated iron and had a rickety door; it was a demarcation rather than a room. The family was not well off, and yet food was always prepared with care. Grandma continued to sob, looking through her Romy Schneider cuttings, and we quietly ate baked pears.

My time in Bordeaux was my second experience of France. The first was an exchange trip, when I was fifteen. The parents in my host family both worked, but every day culminated in a good dinner. The mother would arrive home with fresh pizza dough, ready to be knocked back, finished with a homemade topping and baked; or a friend would turn up for supper with an apricot tart she'd made on her afternoon off.

Cooking was even more important when we went for a month to the father's home village (tiny Lamothe-en-Blaisy, though they called it Lamothe-en-Paradis and it was, indeed, paradise). Every day revolved around the preparation of meals. Clothilde, my counterpart, would start thinking about what to cook for lunch as soon as we'd finished breakfast. Would we do brochettes of lamb? What herb would we put in the vinaigrette today? Salad leaves were carefully washed, then swung in a metal basket outside (the drier the leaves, the better the vinaigrette would cling to them). Provisions were delivered in various vans, the cheesemongers and greengrocers negotiating the dirt tracks that wound between the houses. You could smell the mobile fromagerie before it had parked. I was astonished that the greengrocer sold summer fruits not in paper bags or punnets, as in Britain, but in palettes. At home, my mum counted out strawberries, dividing them equally between me and my siblings; in France, there were glistening tarts piled high with raspberries and people bought stone fruits by the tray.

Clothilde and I spent afternoons at her grandma's going through ancient copies of *Elle*, marking up the dishes we wanted to try. Grandma taught me how to make *tarte aux pommes* with a filling of eggs and crème fraîche; Clothilde's brother showed me how to make perfect crêpes.

I loved supper at their aunt's house. Meals there always began with crudités and charcuterie. This spread, accompanied by baguette with a crust that shattered when you broke it, seemed the best way to start any meal, and Paris-Brest, which was often purchased, the best way to end it. (My love for that caused shameful transgressions. It was kept in the sideboard, under a cloth, and I would steal slivers between lunch and dinner. When I got caught red-handed, the father smiled, '*C'est bon le gâteau, hé Diana?*')

Back at home, my dream of France was nurtured, fed by films – Truffaut, Chabrol and, especially, those of Éric Rohmer (I liked dramas in which nothing happened, except talking and looking and longing) – books and cooking. For years, my notebook of 'dishes to cook' was full of French regional classics, and many of my fantasy meals were served on checked tablecloths with a Jacques Brel soundtrack.

In my twenties, I covered almost the entire country with Patricia Wells's *The Food Lover's Guide to France* as my companion. I read about places I couldn't afford, or that were so out of the way I would never find them. The book sent me to a farm in Normandy where they made their own cider and served it with platters of ham and eggs, and to a hotel with a cupboard housing thirty kinds of jam. In a small inn on the French-Swiss border – where the air smelt of cool grass – I had a cloud of cheese soufflé and perfectly cooked trout for dinner, then couldn't sleep because of the tinkling of cowbells (I lay in the dark, thinking how wonderful it was not to be able to sleep because of the sound of cowbells).

Once I was living in London, the most accessible parts of France were Normandy and Brittany and, later, the coast by La Rochelle. For years, I went to the French seaside at Easter. A trip to Normandy always meant a meal at Les Vapeurs in Trouville, an Art Deco brasserie with paper tablecloths, swift, skinny waiters and teetering towers of *fruits de mer* on avalanches of crushed ice. I couldn't afford the platters then, but I was happy with a pot of mussels cooked in cider, enriched with Normandy cream. Brittany meant buckwheat crêpes, more cider and a wilder coastline. It's a place set apart from the rest of France, harsh and no-nonsense, less romantic. Lunch there was oysters and sourdough from a stall on the roadside, supper a roll-your-sleeves-up affair where you tucked into crevettes and crab claws. The salty tang of seaweed and the aroma of caramelized sugar – from mobile crêperies – hung in the air.

There was a time when good food meant French food. To me it still does, though now you have to know where to find it. In France, as elsewhere, food has become industrialized. The country has lost its influence, partly because, in the area of haute cuisine, Spain flexed its muscles, then the Nordic countries, though western chefs still rely on French technique more than any other. My kitchen, like that of many cooks, is now full of Middle Eastern grains and Asian spices. Travel has opened doors. Interest in food has increased, but at the same time we take the old and the familiar for granted; there's a tendency to love the new, whatever is 'now'.

Classic French food is both simple and complex. The recipes appear to be easy, but you have to pay attention. Dishes have harmony and what the French call *volupté*, meaning they please the senses. A lot of modern food, in contrast, can be cerebral and austere; the elements sit on the plate but don't come together. A good friend, who is a restaurant critic, often says, 'Whatever happened to deliciousness?' Then we daydream about a perfectly dressed green salad, cassoulet and tarte Tatin.

Even though I'd already learned a lot in our kitchen at home in Northern Ireland, France was the first place that showed me the joy that cooking could bring me, both in the process and in the dishes I could put on the table. It pretty much made me a cook.

# 10

# EGGS IS EGGS

Eggs are a miracle of natural architecture: delicate, lovely to hold and somehow complete in themselves. They're relatively cheap, full of protein and perfect for vegetarians and those cutting down on their meat intake. Many of our greatest dishes wouldn't be possible without them. They perform magic. Their yolks provide the base for rich unguents, such as mayonnaise and hollandaise and their various offshoots. They can hold on to air as they set in the heat of an oven, producing clouds of meringue and light-as-a-feather cakes. The eggy filling of a properly cooked quiche can be so delicate it trembles, and a teetering soufflé is a thrill. Now they're the stars of the weekend brunch extravaganza too, sashaying round with all those bottomless jugs of mimosas.

But we usually turn to eggs when we can't think what else to make – I bet your heart sinks when someone says,

'Not much food in the house, I'm afraid. Could always scramble you a couple of eggs' – and we usually cook them badly. Eggs need care. The biggest mistake we make is to apply too fierce a heat. Hot is fine if you're frying an egg and want a frilly edge, but most of the time it just makes eggs rubbery. Scrambled eggs need to be cooked low and slow (adding a knob of butter at the end helps to stop them cooking). A panful of creamy, just-set scrambled eggs is one of the most luxurious things you can eat.

Attention must also be paid to the point at which you stop cooking an omelette. It should never be cooked all the way through, but left *baveuse*, as the French say: slightly uncooked in the centre. You shouldn't boil eggs fiercely either, just at a vigorous simmer, otherwise the shells will crack. When I was ill, my mum used to ask me if I wanted 'a nice boiled egg', or an egg in a cup, shelled, seasoned and mashed with butter. A perfectly boiled egg – white set, yolk soft and running down the side of its cup – is a joy. It's funny that boiling an egg is how we judge someone's culinary competence. 'She can't boil an egg' is not the worst thing you could say of a cook. It's not easy (as Delia Smith knows).

I have to confess to problems with poached eggs. I always lost half the white in the saucepan as it disappeared in little strands. It wasn't until I was taught to poach eggs in a frying pan (where the water is shallower) that

I got it right. Use really fresh eggs – that stops the whites splaying – and very gently simmering water. Crack your egg into a cup, then carefully slide it into the water. For years, I had to make soft-boiled eggs – *des oeufs mollets* – because I found it easier than poaching. These eggs are the crowning glory on many a homely French salad. You have to remove the shell when the egg is cool enough to handle, hold its fragile body over the salad and pierce it, letting its warm yolk run over lentils, hot bacon and bitter leaves. Bliss.

११

# THE WHITE STUFF

I used to loathe yogurt. When I was growing up, the fridge at home was always full of those sour-yet-sickly-sweet little pots of the stuff, that hadn't so much as sniffed a strawberry. My sister, who claimed that eating was boring, could always be prevailed upon to eat a tub of this in lieu of a proper meal, thus confirming my suspicions that the thin, acidic gloop was fit only for people who didn't like food.

Then, as an au pair in France, I discovered set natural yogurt. It came in a blue-and-white carton of minimalist design. *Yaourt nature* had a milky film on top and trembled like a blancmange when you sliced your spoon through it. I was shown how to sprinkle soft dark brown sugar on to the yogurt's surface and let it melt, making a burnt toffee-tasting crust, a sweet piece of which was to be incorporated into every sour mouthful. I would still prefer to eat this than the most perfectly made crème brûlée.

Soon after that, I discovered the luscious Greek stuff. I had made a jar of 'Greek marmalade', a blissful confection of chopped nuts and dried apricots mixed with warm honey and mint, and thought it deserved something better than toast. With Greek yogurt, it made one of those puds whose virtue belies its deliciousness. I couldn't believe that something this rich wasn't as high in fat as double cream (Greek yogurt has one-fifth of double cream's fat content). I'd never liked the airy sweetness of whipped cream anyway, so I embraced this yogurt's tartness, its texture – as creamy as a classy moisturizer – and the way it fell in great thick folds. Greek yogurt made with cow's milk is less tart and more creamy than the ewe's milk version, but both are thick, as they have already been partially strained. I always serve this yogurt, mixed with a little pouring cream and sweetened with icing sugar and vanilla extract, with desserts. The sourness provides the perfect antidote to sugary meringues and sticky toffee pudding and makes an X-rated dessert out of berries and bitter-sweet chocolate cake. It produces a clean, fresh-tasting ice cream, a nice tart pannacotta to go with poached or baked fruit, and, added to custard, a fuller, more balanced base than plain cream for fruit fools.

You won't find little pots of commercial sweetened yogurt in fridges in the Middle East, but big basins of sour, creamy stuff. There, it's as basic a necessity as bread and is used in savoury dishes more than sweet. Yogurt's a sauce, dip, cooking medium and tenderizer. With a little crushed garlic, it makes a moist, soothing cooler that goes well with big fat flavours such as chilli. Dishes of stewed lentils with cumin, lamb pilafs dotted with almonds and apricots and smoky grilled aubergines... they all love the starkness of yogurt. In Iran, where yogurt is particularly popular (it was originally referred to as 'Persian milk' in parts of the Middle East), yogurt dishes even have their own collective name: *boorani* (after Queen Poorandokht, who loved yogurt so much that the royal chefs kept trying out new dishes with it). Such cooling Iranian offerings as spinach and garlic with yogurt, or fried aubergine with yogurt, were invented to please the royal palate. The Turks' *yoğurtlu* dishes use yogurt as a layering ingredient, spreading it over beds of torn pitta to be topped with braised lamb and tomatoes, or sandwiching it between rags of flatbread and hot grilled lamb: the mix of temperatures and textures is delicious.

I also love the crusty, creamy blanket formed when yogurt is mixed with eggs and cheese and baked. The Greeks pour this tart custard over dishes of lamb and vegetables or chicken joints before baking. These make brilliant supper dishes: the best kind of home cooking. Just remember that you need to stabilize the yogurt, which would otherwise split when heated, by adding a little salt and 1 teaspoon of cornflour (mixed to a paste with a little cold water) for every cup of yogurt.

It might seem over the top to make your own yogurt cheese, or labneh, but it's the easiest thing in the world. It simply entails putting thick Greek yogurt into a square of muslin, tying it at the top and hanging it up, or setting it in a sieve, so the whey can run off into a basin or the sink. Even after an hour, the yogurt will have thickened substantially, but I generally leave it for twenty-four hours. I like the sound of the still, slow dripping as something else is formed and it's the nearest I will ever get to the earthy business of cheese-making. It reminds me that milk is a living thing. Unwrapping the yogurt, you find a firm cushion imprinted with the texture of the muslin. It always seems such a pity to break this up, but I do. I put little cold nuggets of it among spicy roast vegetables, or mix it with crushed garlic and salt to make a spread for bread. Strained yogurt's particularly good with sweet slow-roast tomatoes and onions. Or form it into little balls, roll these in paprika or chopped herbs, put them in a jar and cover with olive oil: perfect for mezze. You can also slice your strained yogurt into thick cake-type wedges, leaving the muslin pattern intact, and drizzle it with honey, or a honey-and-flower water syrup. Serve this with sliced fruit: peaches, mangoes or oranges. Healthy but gorgeous.

I use the more runny type of natural yogurt for marinades. Its higher acidity makes it a more effective tenderizer and its liquidity allows it to penetrate the incisions in chicken or lamb. But apart from this, as far as yogurt goes, Greece is the word.

Cheese is almost as important as yogurt in the Middle East and Eastern Mediterranean. The Greeks actually eat more cheese per head than the French every year, hardly surprising when you think it's popular even for breakfast. Apart from labneh, feta-type cheeses (the Turkish version is called *beyaz peynir*) are the most popular and certainly the simplest to make. Once the curds have formed, the whey is drained off and the curds are pressed. When they're firm enough, the curds are salted and left to dry for twenty-four hours before being steeped in brine. After only a month, the cheese is ready to eat and is sold in the manner that gives it its name: *feta* is the Greek word for 'slice'. Though the best examples share a characteristic saltiness, they vary widely in pungency and crumbliness. If you can, buy your feta from a Greek or Turkish deli.

Outside Greece and Turkey, people don't get particularly excited about feta-type cheese, but I love it. Like yogurt cheese, it goes well with sweet things: its tangy crumbs are a great contrast to roast pumpkin, sweet potatoes and roast peppers. Conversely, its sharpness is good with the fresh greenness of cucumber and herbs such as mint, dill and tarragon. Mixed with eggs, herbs and perhaps the sharper *kefalotyri* (a hard Greek cheese that is a bit like Italian pecorino), feta can make endless fillings for Greek filo pies: just add leeks or spinach, pumpkin or chicken, courgettes or aubergines and spoon it into a case of buttered filo leaves. I must say that I also like feta for its texture: it's very satisfying to crumble handfuls of it over a simple Greek lamb and tomato stew, no grating or shaving or any of that malarkey, just a bowl of those little tiny pasta shapes called orzo, and you're away.

I always think ricotta is like a baby cheese; it smells sweetly milky and tastes so mild. It's also unformed, its grainy curds separating when you dig your fork into it. But then, ricotta's hardly a cheese at all; it's a byproduct of cheese-making. Milk is added to the whey that is left over from other cheeses. A little sour whey or some other coagulant is added and the whole thing is heated (hence the name *ricotta* or 're-cooked') until lumps of ricotta form on the surface. Fresh ricotta is creamy white, delicately crumbly and bears as much relation to those plastic tubs of long-life stuff as thick Jersey cream does to UHT. Until you've tasted good ricotta, the point of simple dishes such as pasta with fried courgettes, ricotta and basil will elude you.

The Sicilians, who are often credited with inventing ricotta, adore it, though I can pass on their speciality, cassata. It's an overly sweet baroque fantasy of a cake – layers of sponge, sweetened ricotta and candied fruit topped with pistachio-coloured marzipan – I'd love to like it, but I can't.

But I am happy to mix ricotta with cream and eggs, bitter chocolate and grated orange, or booze-soaked raisins, for a tart filling. Or I'll blend sweetened ricotta and thick cream with lemon zest and juice to fill a sponge. In fact, ricotta is a great 'filler', partly because it's such a good carrier of flavours: spinach, nuts, Parmesan, delicate herbs, nutmeg and flower waters... it perfectly transmits all their nuances.

There are even simpler pleasures, though. Italians make a kind of deconstructed tiramisu by mashing coffee and sugar into ricotta and serving it with sponge fingers. I've often served a bowl of fresh ricotta with dark, sweet cherries. And for a snack, ricotta's good spread on warm ciabatta and sprinkled with olive oil and basil leaves.

The best thing about yogurt, feta and ricotta is their purity, their simple clean flavours. They're enjoyable without undergoing any cooking. I'll happily breakfast on bread spread with strained yogurt and honey; I'll snack on a chunk of feta with olives and herbs; I'll have a lunch of ricotta with extra virgin olive oil and vegetables; or finish a meal with a mound of ricotta mashed with crushed raspberries and sugar. With ingredients this good, you can eat well without cooking.

## 12

# HEAVEN SCENT

I fell for the idea of eating flowers when I was six. At a school bring-and-buy sale, there was a raffle for a cake. It was tiered, covered in thick creamy white icing and adorned with a cascade of fragrant, deep-red rose petals and half-closed buds. I was mesmerized – this was a cake for Snow White – and I couldn't fill my nostrils enough with its scent. I felt like the only way to capture this aroma was to eat the cake. But we didn't win the raffle. Someone else carried away the promise of consuming those velvet flowers.

By chance, the present bought to ease this disappointment was my first bottle of perfume: a little china capsule of African violets. I kept sniffing it. I could taste the scent and I really wanted to eat its purpleness.

For many people, the idea of flowers and their fragrance conjures up images of an English afternoon tea – a sweet little cake dotted with crystallized petals to match the china cups – or the musty corners of Granny's handbag. The whole notion is cosy, cute, even a little cloying. Not me. I have always felt that the subtlety of petals and their scent rendered them uncapturable and hence mysterious and desirable. I couldn't devour those violets the way I would a chocolate bar... and I wanted to.

As far as violets go, I was right; their aroma is literally evanescent. Violets contain ionones, chemicals that temporarily short-circuit our sense of smell, so their fragrance comes and goes in bursts. You can't drink in the scent the way you want to. But roses and orange blossom seem ephemeral too. That is the magic of floral fragrances. Your nose can follow them like your eyes would follow a piece of silk as it darts through a network of alleyways. When you taste them, the flavour still eludes you, as if you are eating a piece of a place that might not exist, or a memory of something that never really happened.

And I'm not the only one who feels like this; few things over the centuries have tantalized and seduced like scents. The ancient Persians made wine from rose petals, the Romans strewed their floors with them, Cleopatra anointed her hands with oil of roses, crocus and violets and Napoleon – even during his toughest campaigns – took time to choose between rose- and violet-scented finery. Forget Granny's cupboards, think Antony and Cleopatra making love on a bed of petals, Roman diners being sprayed with flower waters between courses and gladiators rubbing oil of flowers into their loins.

Now, in an age when the most far-flung spices have been made familiar by supermarkets and takeaways, the smell of blossoms in our saucepans is one of the few scents that can still transport us. Both rose water and orange flower water are used all over the Middle East and North Africa. Pastries are drenched in blossom-scented sugar syrups and rose petal jam is eaten at breakfast, or as a 'spoon sweet' served at afternoon tea with tinkling silver spoons, cups of strong coffee and little glasses of iced water.

A tablespoon of orange flower water stirred into a cup of boiling water is known as a *café blanc* in Lebanon, while drops of flower water added to Persian fruit and meat stews – *khoresht* – lend them a haunting, indefinable flavour. Dried rose petals are part of the Persian spice mix advieh, in which they join cinnamon, cardamom and cumin, and the petals are also added to the classic North African spice blend ras al hanout.

Flowers have been used for years to flavour sharbats, the sugary syrups that are the base of cold drinks made all over the Middle East. As Claudia Roden writes in *A New Book of Middle Eastern Food*, remembering the cries of the sharbat sellers in the Cairo of her childhood: 'The vendors carried a selection of sherbets in gigantic glass flasks... The flasks glowed with brilliantly seductive colours: soft, pale, sugary pink for rose water, pale green for violet juice, warm, rich, dark tamarind and the purple-black of mulberry juice.'

No-one is certain whether it was Arab sharbats that eventually metamorphosed into the ice creams of Naples and Sicily but, when the Arabs were in power, snow was brought from Etna to ice these drinks. Perhaps it wasn't much of a leap from near-frozen sharbat to granita, and, eventually, sorbet. In any case, you can still find orange blossom and jasmine ice creams in Sicily, and Middle Eastern ice cream flavoured with rose water is one of the most sublime tastes in the world, just subtle enough to be like eating spoonfuls of a summer that is past.

The great thing is that these drops of flavour are quite attainable. Middle Eastern and Indian groceries stock orange flower water, made from the blossom of the Seville orange, as well as rose water, and it's not difficult to get hold of a handful of fragrant unsprayed rose petals.

American chef Jerry Traunfeld, who cooked until recently at The Herbfarm restaurant near Seattle, specialized in cooking with herbs and flowers. He made floral syrups by whizzing petals and sugar in a food processor before adding water and boiling to a sticky, limpid liquid. Those were used for fruit salads and as a base for sorbets. The sugars last for ages; just keep them in a screw-top jar and add them to whipped cream or fruit fools, sift over fruit-topped meringues, or use them in cake batter or to make a buttercream filling.

All rose petals, as long as they haven't been sprayed with pesticides, are quite edible, but they differ enormously in their smell and taste. The modern hybrid tea roses have been bred for form rather than for fragrance, so use the old-fashioned, flat, full-blossoming roses, which are much more heady. If you're going to make rose jam, or something that needs a lot of rose petals, it is best to either befriend a sympathetic gardener or to grow them yourself, but you can impart enough rose fragrance to most things with flower water or, if they're heavily scented enough, a few blooms. Try throwing a handful of petals over the fruit in a cherry pie before baking it, or making a punch from a bottle of rosé Champagne, a little cassis and a glug of rose water; float strawberries and rose petals on top and you have a drink that could be served at the wedding feast in *A Midsummer Night's Dream*.

Rose water has a wonderful affinity with red summer fruits, but try using it as they do in the Middle East, too: add it to poached apples in the winter, or chilled, grated apples or melon in the summer. Both rose water and orange flower water transport milk puddings: a little orange flower water and a few pods of crushed cardamom can take a plain old rice pudding to the shores of the Bosphorus in one delicious mouthful.

Orange flower water tastes good with golden-coloured fruits – peaches, nectarines, mangoes and apricots – and really enhances almonds, so stick it into cakes, tarts and biscuits for a little perfume of Provence, where it's also popular. Use a lighter hand than you do with rose water, or it can become rather sickly, though to be honest I could drink the stuff. I can never smell orange flower water without simultaneously smelling the scents of fresh mint and coriander, the smell of markets in Morocco. If you like scents for their power to transport you, orange flower water is a rocket. When I've been baking a lot with it, scattering it over little pastries, my kitchen and my skin breathe Morocco.

Violets are much more English and much less versatile. They're used for those violet fondant creams so beloved of the late Queen Mother, but they don't turn up much in the Middle East. The French have a penchant for them, though. In Toulouse, they've been growing the heavily scented Parma violets since the 1850s, turning them into jam – the delicate petals suspended in a translucent mauve jelly – and, of course, crystallizing the heads. There's even a violet liqueur that looks wickedly purple, but smells innocently sweet. The jam and the crystallized flowers are easy to pick up in specialist food stores in France, but you'll have to find an enterprising food emporium or specialist spirit merchant for the liqueur.

The aroma of violets is certainly more cloying than that of orange blossom or roses, the kind of overly sweet scent that schoolgirls fall for. In fact, I used to stand in my school uniform in the sweet shop, passing my pocket money from one hot hand to the other, torn between the perfumed romance of a packet of Parma Violets (a cellophane-wrapped tube of lilac-coloured buttons) and the adult sophistication of a bar of Fry's Chocolate Cream. It's a shame you couldn't have mixed the two: the taste of violets is wonderful with both white and dark chocolate. Try adding a few drops of violet liqueur to the glaze or filling for a chocolate cake.

Violets are good with strawberries, raspberries and apricots, too. Wines made from the viognier grape are often described as having the scents of both violets and apricots, so I suppose that the pairing isn't really surprising. Add just a dash of violet liqueur to the syrup in which you have poached apricots, or to a bowl of cream to be served alongside.

Using flowers in food won't be to everyone's taste, but the power scents have to evoke memories and a sense of place makes them an irresistible ingredient. A couple of bottles of flower water and a few handfuls of petals will turn you into a perfumier as well as a cook, with the art of catering for the most complex of senses as well as the most basic.

# WATERMELON FOR BREAKFAST

We're dragging our luggage across the lobby when the hotel owner spots my seven-year-old. As we sign the register, he rings the little brass bell that sits on the reception desk and Turkish delight – a sugar-dusted pyramid of it in a stemmed dish – arrives. My son's eyes are so wide with wonder, he might as well have stumbled into the snows of Narnia. This is the kind of warmth you find in Istanbul. It's a big city – the population has grown from two million to fourteen million in the last twenty-five years – but constant acts of kindness make it feel like a village. Spiced apple tea and pastries are delivered to our room and we sit on the tiny terrace, a stone's throw from the Blue Mosque, devouring baklava and blue skies.

Istanbul, for me, is summed up by the colour blue. I've only been there under summer skies, never in winter; the only item I bought on my first visit was a blue shawl

– the colour of the Iznik tiles that decorate so many of Istanbul's interiors – for covering my head when visiting mosques. And then there's the Bosphorus, the blue water dividing and joining the two sides of the city, European and Asian, its two worlds. Blue is an optimistic colour; it means horizons and space, skies and seas. I feel, in Istanbul, that I can stretch out my arms and touch the rest of the world.

The city is at the edge of everything, and the world also comes to it. Sit in a rickety teahouse by the Bosphorus and you can see it, boats and ferries and tankers from Norway and Italy and Cambodia – even warships from Russia – churning up the water, while smaller vessels bravely steer a course among them (ship counting and serious ship-spotting are Istanbul pastimes).

The food here is at the meeting point of lots of cultures, too. On the surface it seems simple; most meals start with vegetables, cucumbers as juicy and taut as apples, firm chilled radishes, lengths of scarlet pepper. The counterpoints to these are tart or salty, the snow-white cheese *beyaz peynir*, clouds of pale creamy-pink tarama, bowls of thick yogurt. The tarama is a dish shared with the Balkans and Greece.

But look beyond these; *acuka*, a purée of red peppers, walnuts, garlic, tomato and chilli, is Syrian in origin; the chicken coated with a creamy walnut and garlic sauce is from Circassia; *manti*, little dumplings stuffed with spiced lamb and smothered in yogurt, are thought to have come to Turkey along the Silk Road from Central Asia. There are influences from all over the former Ottoman Empire: the Middle East, the Balkans, the Caucasus and parts of North Africa.

You think you know, or have at least read about, all the preparations for aubergines and lamb, and then you visit Çiya Sofrası in Kadıköy, probably the best and most-loved restaurant on the Asian shore, and one that has been described as 'a garden of lost cultures and forgotten tastes'. Here the owner, Musa Dağdeviren, is trying to document, restore and maintain Turkish dishes that could otherwise get left behind; you don't recognize many of them, neither the cold mezze on one side of the restaurant, nor the contents of the bubbling pots on the other (and my *Istanbullu* friends tell me it's often the same for them). Much of the food is in shades of deep purple or green: lamb with plums, melting aubergines slick with pomegranate molasses, pilaf with mulberries, fat glossy stuffed vine leaves. You choose your mezze and pay for the plate by weight, take it to your table and try to work out which flavours – cumin, sumac, or pul biber – are playing across each other. There are some ingredients, though – milk thistle, hyssop – that you probably won't guess correctly.

Food is taken very seriously in Istanbul, but not because it's cool. Offering people good food is a tenet of faith (it's a command of the Prophet) even among those who hold none. Its importance was signalled from the earliest days of the Ottoman Empire. When Sultan Mehmed II conquered Constantinople in the 15th century, he built the Topkapı Palace with a huge four-domed kitchen. More domes and sections were added until the kitchens, at their peak (when feeding guests and visiting diplomats), housed nearly 1,400 cooks. It was a furnace of culinary creativity: new dishes were developed, Byzantine recipes were adopted and updated, and ingredients from every part of the Empire were used. Imagine the discussions, the excitement when chillies arrived, or unfamiliar varieties of grape. Cooking was respected, considered an art; poets and musicians composed poems and sang songs about it and every wealthy household in the city tried to keep up with the standards set in the Topkapı.

The Palace kitchens were separated into specialist sections – pastry, milk puddings, halvah, drinks, even pickles – and when Turkey became a secular Republic in 1923, the cooks lost their jobs. Many of them went abroad, but the idea of specialisms continued. In markets today you can see picklers and preservers, their green figs and pink-tinged florets of cauliflower glowing behind glass, and the *muhallebicisi*, or 'milk pudding-makers' (the very idea of being a milk pudding-maker, provider of sweetness and comfort) have small, simple restaurants, though most now sell pastries and other snacks as well as milk puddings. In these, you can have *muhallebi*, soft, just-set squares of milk pudding made with rice flour, *tavukgöğsü*, an ancient dish of poached chicken breast pounded with milk, rice flour, sugar and cinnamon, and *aşure*, a wheat pudding made with nuts and dried fruits. These dishes are often fragrant with mastic, a translucent resin that tastes slightly of pine and cedar, or flower waters.

What is so seductive about the food in Istanbul is the blending – an accident of history – of simple nomadic dishes and staples with the remnants of the more sophisticated palace cuisine. It's rich and layered and there's a place to eat every kind of food at all different times of the day. There are rooftop cocktail bars with glittering views; *kebapçı*, where you can spend half an hour trying to choose which of twenty-five kebabs you're going to order; or street food stalls that lure you with the charred oiliness of mackerel and the slightly sweet smell of *simit*, sesame-flecked bracelets of bread.

Turks love a big breakfast: vegetables, cheese, figs and watermelon along with jams, yogurt and honey, which is a mere precursor to mid-morning coffee. Then there's lunch, taken in one of the many *lokantas* (simple taverns or 'canteens'). As late afternoon approaches, I wonder if I'll have pastries and tea, or sherbet (sweet cordials made from mint, sour cherries, quince or lemons) or ice cream... I check every ice cream shop I see, looking for the unusual, mulberry or tahini, though I can always depend on a little tub of rose ice cream flavoured with salep, dried and ground orchid root. Then it's mezze and raki before dinner.

The Turkish novelist Orhan Pamuk has written about *hüzün*, the melancholy (which can be painful, but also enjoyable, because it is shared) that he and other *Istanbullus* feel. It might be engendered simply by rain on a window, or the sad weak light that gathers at the end of a winter afternoon. But *hüzün* is also a sense of loss, the result of being born into a city 'buried under the ashes of a ruined empire'. I do not feel this melancholy. It is not mine to feel. If I'm in Istanbul during Ramadan, when the area around the Blue Mosque is full of picnickers spreading out cloths on the ground and hungrily eating *börek* and *lahmacun* at midnight, I can't even see it. I just see generosity and beauty and joy.

I used to play a game, when I first started travelling in my late teens. I would ask myself, 'Could you live here if you had to?' I was testing my independence. I have never stopped playing this game. The first time I rode the ferry from one side of the Bosphorus to the other, going to the Asian shore with the end-of-day commuters – talking loudly, eating peaches, reading – I watched the water become a great white spume behind the boat and asked myself this question. I looked at the skyline with its domes and rocket-like minarets, its mix of old and modern, and thought: oh yes. But I want an apartment with a view, however small a fragment, of the blue Bosphorus, and a good café nearby where I can start every day with salty cheese and melon.

# 14
# PASTA

August in Rome. I'm sitting in a quiet trattoria in the suburbs. It has taken an hour to get here in the sweltering heat, but it's worth it: the place is famous for its *fritti* – arancini, as well as courgette flowers stuffed with cheese and anchovies – and its pasta. As soon as the carbonara, a dish in which eggs are cooked just enough by strands of hot spaghetti to form a 'sauce' (but not so much that they scramble) arrives, I am completely content. I'm also reminded how good something this ordinary and inexpensive – only the nuggets of salty guanciale with which the dish is studded cost much – can be. It isn't just the flavour, it's the fact that it's soft, that there is a ritual to eating it – twirling it round your fork – that it can be made quickly and with a little style.

I watch the Italians around me eating small platefuls of pasta as a precursor to their *pollo alla diavola* or veal chop... and think of my favourite pasta photographs, of Maria Callas and a group of her girlfriends eating pasta on a train in 1955 on the way to La Scala, of Sophia Loren looking for all the world as if pasta had created every wonderful curve on her body. They are all eating with such joy, heads held back and mouths wide open, as though a love of pasta exhibits a love of life itself.

Most of us, in contrast, have come to regard pasta not as a joy, but as a filler. It's the convenience food *par excellence*; it's easy and nearly every child will eat it. God knows what we did before supermarkets were full of packets of tubes, strands, shells, corkscrews and butterflies. Familiarity has, to a certain extent, bred contempt.

For a start, we don't prepare it well. Pasta has to be cooked in plenty of boiling salted water (1 litre/1¾ pints for every 100g/3½oz of pasta). Dress it with melted butter or olive oil if your sauce isn't ready and, when saucing, don't overdo it; the pasta, with its own flavour and texture, is just as important as the sauce. Remember that the sauce should just coat the pasta, not drown it. Adding a little of the cooking water from the pasta to the sauce loosens it, and helps both pasta and sauce to combine well.

Tossed with cream, lemon zest and shreds of Parma ham, or with wild mushrooms and truffles, pasta can be luxurious, but more often it allows you to revel in the frugal... and also to cook spontaneously. I feel a little rise of pleasure as I spot a bunch of parsley that can be tossed with spaghetti, extra virgin olive oil and dried chilli. Carrying a big bowl of this to the table makes me happy: I've taken ordinary ingredients and turned them into something good.

Frugal, simple, generous, these are some of the best attributes a dish can have (in my book, anyway). Pasta, if cooked with care and approached with verve, can be all these things, something that Maria Callas and Sophia Loren knew well.

# AFTER THE *PASSEGGIATA*

Southern Italy is the Italy of the Northern European imagination. I grew up, in a Northern Irish seaside town, visiting an ice cream parlour – Morelli's – that had a picture of the Amalfi coast running along one wall. I was mesmerized, at six years old, that such a place could exist. The sea was cobalt blue, the flowers scarlet. It was so unlike the choppy, pewter Atlantic the café looked out over.

When I eventually got to the South of Italy, as an adult, it was all I had hoped for and more. Amalfi, Sorrento and Ravello, with their terraces of citrus trees and floods of bougainvillea, all linked by a cliff-hugging ribbon of road, are patchworks of colour, light and stone. At least, they are in the warmer months. My first trip there was to a wintry Amalfi. The lemon trees were wrapped in grey gauze to protect them from hailstones – making them look like ghosts – and the sea was dark and angry.

Over the years, the Southern Italy I have come to love more is far from the carefree, monied ease of Ravello; it is more chaotic, muscular, vigorous and poorer. Naples, where the air smells of coffee, fried dough and the sea; Sicily, where they eat ice cream and brioche for breakfast; Polignano a Mare in Puglia, where the *passeggiata* feels like a festival (the *passeggiata*, an evening promenade, is about showing off and letting go of the day, giving a damn and yet not giving a damn).

Your first hour in Naples makes you wonder what drug you've been slipped. It's both frightening and exhilarating. You feel it might implode and you have no idea, at first, how to find its centre, and I don't mean its physical centre, but its emotional one. The city seems unmappable, unknowable. There's noise – shouting, car horns, the throaty gurgle of the Vespas that perilously take every street corner – and activity (gossiping, drinking, smoking) everywhere. Small streets criss-cross and veer off at odd angles, slivers of sea float into view when you least expect them, then disappear, cars are parked almost on top of each other, vendors (often elderly ladies wrapped in shawls) sell motley collections of goods: lighters, plastic toys and mysterious liqueurs. There are layers – of hanging laundry, of crumbling plaster, of paint and posters and history – and colours appear saturated. It can be hard to work out where to focus.

Strategic and beautiful, Naples has been fought over and colonized by Greeks, Romans, Normans and Spanish. It has seen it all and survived and its fighting spirit is evident. It's not a place for ritzy restaurants; you eat on the hoof, grabbing a slice of pizza, then, later, a *sfogliatella* (a shell-shaped layered pastry stuffed with ricotta and candied peel) or an ice cream.

There has been complex, aristocratic cooking here. Queen Maria Carolina de Bourbon, Marie-Antoinette's sister, brought French chefs to her court in the 18th century, to inject some sophistication. These chefs, known as *monzus* (a corruption of monsieur) fused down-to-earth Neapolitan food, such as macaroni, with French complexity. Today it's hard to see that influence, though you find babas in pastry shops and crème pâtissière (*crema pasticcera*) is used.

Now, the cooking of Naples, and all of Southern Italy, is direct, intense and imaginative, the product of the genius of home cooks, who need to make the best of vegetables, pasta, pulses, bread and leftovers. They know how to turn breadcrumbs into something so delicious (frying them until golden, crunchy and perfumed with olive oil and garlic) that you eat them on pasta and don't miss Parmesan. Then there's leftover risotto, formed into cones or balls, stuffed with cheese or ragù and deep-fried until they are simultaneously soothing and explosive.

Limitations can be a powerfully creative force; they encourage care. If you only have tomatoes, garlic, onions and olive oil you will work out how to make the best tomato sauce, even slightly different versions according to your mood or the time of year. That's partly why you can eat pasta with tomato sauce in Southern Italy and marvel at its depth.

Sometimes it seems wrong to rhapsodize about what is essentially a *cucina povera*. We forget the actual poor. This hit me when I got lost in Palermo years ago. In a cramped residential area, I stumbled across an old woman sitting in a small garage: her home. There was an old wrought-iron bed with a stained mattress, bags of clothes, a gas stove with a coffee pot. She sat in a plastic deckchair and around her, on the ground, was the peel of a dozen or more oranges. She was still greedily eating them and offered one to me. Sicilian oranges are some of the best in the world, but they're probably not so great if they're the only thing you have to eat.

As well as care, ordinary ingredients need strong flavours to make them seductive, the flavours of peperoncini (*la droga dei poveri*, 'the drug of the poor'), garlic, oregano, cured anchovies, capers... But you can also find the mild and the gentle here. In Puglia, burrata (which means 'buttery') oozes cream and smells of new milk. Slice tomatoes or ripe peaches and eat them with this, black pepper, salt and extra virgin olive oil. Why would you cook? In Sicily, you can buy ricotta that's still warm, the curds just holding together, sitting in its basket like a newborn milky wonder (it's hard not to scoop it up on your fingers and eat it as you cook). The last time I was there, I cooked green beans, tossed them with oil, lemon juice and chilli and put little nuggets of ricotta on top. It was the best thing I ate.

Apart from the simplicity of Southern Italian food, I love the Arab legacy. Not only did they bring ingredients – citrus trees and sugar and aubergines – but they brought their blending of savoury with sweet, which you see so clearly in the food of Sicily. There's also a mad passion for the sweet and the decorative (though food historians can't agree whether this is from the Arabs or not), including fruits and animals made from marzipan. They're most in evidence in Sicily. One Easter, I watched Corrado Costanzo, owner of one of the island's most famous *gelaterie*, sculpt these with his large hands. With turns and flicks of his wrist, lumps of marzipan were transformed – he used only a few small tools, then applied colour with tiny brushes – into doll-sized lemons and blushing apricots. They appeared so fluidly, I was sure he must be performing some sleight of hand.

They have a saying in Naples, 'It doesn't matter whether we're governed by France or Spain so long as we eat,' and you get that sense all over Southern Italy. There's a hedonism – it may have developed out of a simple need for self-preservation – that seems like a good attitude to me. Negronis aren't a Southern Italian drink – Campari and other bitter drinks were created in the back rooms of bars in Northern Italy – but it's my favourite way to kick off any Italian meal. Pour yourself one before anyone arrives. Hedonism, remember...

# 16
# I HATED SUNDAY LUNCH

As a teenager, I hated Sunday lunch. My parents usually called on friends at midday, leaving me to cook the vegetables (the meat – an excellent bit of Irish beef – was already in the oven). I was a good cook, but there was something about the grinding dullness of this task, and the fact that I tried to combine it with homework, that made me wilfully incapable of pulling it off. Sunday after Sunday I would let the carrots boil dry, then try to get rid of the smell while prising the burnt batons off the saucepan.

When I was an au pair in France, I went to a Sunday lunch that made me feel as though I was appearing in a Truffaut film. 'That's the way to do it,' I thought. My host Agnes lived with her husband and children in a dilapidated farmhouse. The Sunday lunch in question wasn't grand, but the whole thing was pulled off with style and grace. We drank chilled Pineau des Charentes and picked at charcuterie, then sat down at a table dressed with a simple white cloth and ate roast lamb with *petits pois à la française* and artichoke hearts (I remember my shock at the absence of potatoes). Afterwards, there was a green salad – using just one kind of leaf – with a good dressing; one perfect cheese; and poached peaches. What was special about this meal is that it was unremarkable. There was no endless procession of vegetables and desserts, no complicated dishes. It was chic in its simplicity; served on platters and in big serving bowls, it felt generous and inclusive.

It took me years to approach anything like the ideal of Agnes's lunch. I loved the idea of a laid-back Sunday lunch, but would always make too many dishes or serve enough desserts to put on a small trolley. When I asked my partner's parents to Sunday lunch for the first time, I actually managed to singe my hair while juggling too many pans. I was able to snip the burnt bit off, but the smell rather gave me away…

Here are some guidelines for a relaxed Sunday lunch: no starter, you're not running a restaurant. Charcuterie, olives and radishes are as far as you should go. Have ice, decent gin or some other apéritif, but remember you're not kitting out a bar. Offer no more than two side dishes (one should be easy to make). One pudding is enough.

(Though that's hard advice to follow. I always have a fruit pudding – my favourite – and somehow Sunday lunch is a great place for some old-fashioned stodge such as bread-and-butter pudding.) If you can't be bothered to make pudding at all, a bottle of dessert wine is fine.

It's difficult to resist the temptation to offer lots of choice, after all it seems generous. But with Sunday lunch, as with so many things, less is more. Keep it simple.

/ 7

# THE SNARE OF SUGAR

Love can make you do crazy things. I once took an enormous detour while driving to the South of France – making a dog-leg through the Loire Valley when I was actually heading for Menton – because of my love of jam. The *Good Hotel Guide* had a description of a rather eccentric hotel in Chinon whose main pull was an armoire housing thirty flavours of jam.

I fantasized about that cupboard for weeks. The idea of those jewel-coloured jars arranged on old wooden shelves was more alluring than the prospect of my holiday on the Côte d'Azur. Breakfast time at the Hôtel Diderot arrived, the armoire was flung open, and there they were: apricot, cherry, redcurrant, peach and raspberry, green fig... you name it, they had it. The sight was exhilarating. No-nonsense girls in black skirts and white aprons distributed croissants, tartines and... just two flavours of jam.

We had driven miles and not tasted twenty-eight of the flavours. Manners got me another two, but I was gutted.

Simone de Beauvoir compared jam-making to the capturing of time: 'The housewife has caught duration in the snare of sugar, she has enclosed life in jars.' I like the idea of stopping a fruit dead in its tracks so you can eke it out little by little (though certainly wouldn't restrict jam-making to housewives). But preserving is also about capturing and holding on to a season, a particular mood. You can find autumn in a jar of pear and chestnut jam, or the fragrance of your Provençal summer holiday in a pot of apricot and lavender. It is one of the most poetic branches of cookery.

I started making jam relatively late in my culinary life. Until then, it had seemed a little daunting, reserved for the serious preserver with gleaming equipment and days at her disposal. Once you start, though, it quickly becomes easy. Now, I sometimes make just a few pots at a time; you don't have to have a full-on session.

There are key things to know – how to get a set, how certain fruits behave, how to sterilize jars and equipment – but it's not rocket science. And getting to grips with the science doesn't preclude creativity. The more often you make jam, the more you know what is possible and you soon start inventing your own flavours. It is also fine, as I learned in Scandinavia, to bend the rules, to make 'jams' like fruit purées. Indeed, I make three different kinds of strawberry jam: an old-fashioned sweet, thick jam; another lower in sugar that needs to be kept in the fridge; and a final type which is pretty much a sweet purée (delicious, as long as you don't mind it running off your scones). They are all good in different ways.

Jam-making has traditionally been seen as the domain of ladies of a certain age. But even if you're on the right side of forty, have a go. You'll think it's worth it every time your toast pops, and greedy friends, children, husbands and boyfriends will love it.

# 18

# THE STREETS OF SAN FRANCISCO

On a rainy afternoon in 1985, I walked into a bookshop in North London and found a volume that has moved between my bedside table, desk and kitchen ever since. It was the *Chez Panisse Menu Cookbook*, by Alice Waters. I knew who Waters was – I'd read about her restaurant in Berkeley – but I didn't know much about her cooking style. British food lovers, at that time, were in thrall to nouvelle cuisine. We were buying hexagonal plates and reducing litres of veal stock (I regularly carried three stone of veal bones home on the Tube). Chefs pushed tiny diamonds of red pepper into position with tweezers. The dishes were complex and the menu descriptions ('pillows of fish mousse nestling in a nage') ludicrous.

    I stood and leafed through the Chez Panisse menus – baked garlic with goat's cheese, charcoal-grilled pork with roasted peppers, plum sherbet – and my spine tingled. I felt as if I'd plunged into the sea, such was the freshness of this food. I could immediately taste it and see it. It was bold because it was simple, and it had a kind of magic. For Alice, a bowl of fresh cherries with homemade almond biscuits was a good dessert. I immediately understood this woman.

Furthermore, Alice, like me, loved menus. Chez Panisse served a set dinner every day. This gave the cooking a definite style, a clarity. Alice understood the importance of a well-dressed salad, too, the dish I learned to value more than any other during my own time in France. People have often said that Alice cooked Californian produce with a Mediterranean sensibility. In fact, her approach was shaped by living in Paris. It wasn't the sun that was important, but the care with which food was cooked, the importance placed on ingredients, the way producers (farmers, growers, bakers) were valued. I'd already taken this message from home – it was something I grew up with – but as you cook it's easy to lose your way.

For years when I felt this was happening, when I was trying to do tricksy things (like getting two sauces to meet in a line on the plate), or was being seduced by some fad, I went back to the *Chez Panisse Menu Cookbook*. I only needed to read a few of the menus and I'd be back on track. It was my lodestar.

I visited Chez Panisse for the first time in 1992; it was the highlight of a meticulously planned American food trip: three weeks, eating in restaurants I'd dreamed about for years. I sat across the road in the car for half an hour just looking at Chez Panisse before I went in. Inside it was all candles and glowing wood. The meal – salt cod gratin, grilled lamb with black olives, Marsala-baked pears – was everything I had hoped for: great ingredients, nothing extraneous. I still have the menu. I ate in other places that week, and discovered how many chefs had passed through the Chez Panisse kitchen, taking its philosophy with them. I ate the late Judy Rodger's roast chicken at Zuni Café and a Mediterranean feast from Joyce Goldstein at Square One. I bought so many books by Californian chefs that I had to buy an extra suitcase for them. What I saw and ate in that short period – again and again – was an honesty, a kind of plain and simple beauty. Cooks here cared about a perfect goat's cheese and a good roast chicken, in the same way as the French did, but their food had more energy; there was also more diversity in California – Asian and Mexican food as well as Mediterranean – and the ingredients, the lemons and figs and melons, seemed more intense.

Back in London, I held on to my San Francisco connection via books. I cooked from them, of course, and while in Books for Cooks, the tiny bookshop I visited often, I was always to be found in the American section.

When I eventually gave up my job as a television producer and started to write, I sent my first book, *Crazy Water, Pickled Lemons*, to Joyce Goldstein, the most Mediterranean- and North Africa-loving of the three San Francisco chefs I most admired. I didn't expect to hear from her, but she loved the book and wrote to me. This started a communication that has gone on ever since. Over the years, she has sent me her books and I've sent her mine. We met – finally – when I was in the States on a publicity tour. She held a dinner for me in San Francisco; I had to go and have a cry halfway through.

I finally realized only last year, while deep in conversation with Alice about her memoir, what had really got to me thirty years before about the whole Northern Californian Chez Panisse philosophy. It was the care they all took – over the typeface used for the menus, the candles, the flowers, the crockery, the produce – it was about valuing the ordinary, seeing the beauty in the small things. It was about caring that you can buy good cherries – that everyone can – and knowing that serving these cherries to friends is a good thing, just because they're beautiful and they taste good.

Alice kept using the word 'love' in her memoir, not just about people, but about all sorts of things: early evening light, candles, mulberry ice cream, hats, peaches. She is a sensualist, as are all the Californian chefs I admire.

They notice everything that you can see and taste and smell. And their lives are richer for it. I think this is what I immediately picked up on in that book shop. The *Chez Panisse Menu Cookbook* is not just a cookbook, it is a way of seeing things, which is why I keep going back to it.

I know it seems strange – this Northern Irish woman cleaving to a West Coast approach to food and to life – but when Joyce Goldstein gave that dinner, I felt I was absolutely in the right place. And when she stood up and said that my books made me an honorary Californian, a San Franciscan cook, it was the highest compliment she could have paid me.

# 19
# TOAST

Toast is essentially a private pleasure, not something we often serve to others (except at breakfast). It's also, for me, the go-to emotional food. If I'm unhappy, I think I deserve toast. When I feel tired and need a pick-me-up, I wait for a slice of sourdough to pop. When I had post-natal depression, toast with lots of butter was the only food that could over-ride my lack of appetite and break through the bleakness. That makes it special.

I'm not alone in my ardour. Toast is a British love. Chewy, warm and slightly nutty, it's the mother of all comfort foods, a friend in good times and in bad.

Now that we take bread more seriously, we are beginning to think toast more important, too. As long as you use good bread and top it with something that has the healthy seal of approval (nut butter, crushed avocado, local honey), it's mandatory to show off your toast via

Instagram. When I met Apollonia Poilâne, whose family produce the world-famous Poilâne sourdough, she served me a feast of... toast, explaining that sourdough actually tastes best several days after baking, toasted, as this brings out its characteristic tang.

A few years back, San Franciscans – as is their wont – went all hipster about toast. Critics touted the $3 slice of artisanal toast as proof that this food-obsessed city had become a parody of itself. But they were doing good things with it. Cafés developed 'toast bar' menus, and every time I visited a classy American food website, someone had come up with a new twist on avo toast.

We Brits can claim a greater toast history than Californians, though. We've been putting interesting things on toast since the Middle Ages ('pokerounce', toast topped with hot honey, ginger and cinnamon, sounds particularly good, as does quince purée with flower water). Then there are 'savouries', specifically English treats of toast topped with anchovies, grated cheese or ham and served at the end of dinner, so beloved of the Victorians and Edwardians.

Food historian Dr Annie Gray says we love toast because we have such a big bread culture in Britain. 'Toast is a sensible way of using the remains of the loaf from the day before: it's thrifty. The kind of bread we like here lasts quite well, too, unlike French baguette which is basically so hard the day after it's made, it's impossible to do anything with it.'

Now toast has become the basis for a decent meal again: a proper lunch, a nourishing supper. It's especially useful if you're on your own, or there are just two of you. There are no rules about preparing it, though you should use good bread. Cheap sliced bread made by the Chorleywood method will be pappy inside; you want a toasted exterior and a good fluffy interior. It's also best to stand your newly toasted slice up against something so it cools just slightly before adding your topping. This prevents sogginess. And you wouldn't want that.

# 20

# CRUMBS

I hate throwing bread away. There seems such potential in it, and I'm very aware what a fundamental foodstuff it is: the staff of life. In North Africa, it's the one food that will be eagerly retrieved if dropped, then wiped and kissed – it is so prized – yet most of us chuck out the end of a loaf without a second thought. But it's worth considering what you can do with that bit. Using bread well means you can afford to pay a little more for better-quality loaves.

I used to baulk at the price of good sourdough, but if you use it all, you've had the pleasure of bread that is both worth eating and makes you feel fuller. If you don't believe me, compare how you feel after eating a bit of good coarse country bread from a bakery to how you feel after a slice of the sorry processed stuff that passes for bread in Britain.

Once bread has lost its soft freshness, it passes through different phases. It can be toasted – good toast is a glorious edible platter – but it doesn't end there. A stuffing made from breadcrumbs is the most obvious way to use old bread, and sage and onion is just the start. Go Caribbean and mix breadcrumbs with lime zest, thyme, spring onion, chilli and rum and use it to stuff a chicken, or toss breadcrumbs with sautéed aubergine, dates and coriander for a Middle Eastern-inspired filling for lamb. You just need enough fat (butter or oil) to bind and keep the bread moist. Roasted tomatoes, aubergines, peppers and mushrooms can all be enhanced by crumbs.

The popularity of 'peasant cooking' has seen us exalt dishes that were created specifically to use up leftover bread. There's the Italian bread salad, panzanella (the Italians are good at counting every crumb), bread-and-butter pudding, pain perdu, summer pudding and spaghetti with fried crumbs. Bread's ability to soak up other flavours, to be soft or crispy, to thicken without altering the character of a dish, make it one of the most useful leftovers. See that sausage and bean casserole that isn't rib-sticking enough, or that puréed mushroom soup that is a bit thin? Throw in a handful of breadcrumbs and watch these dishes come together.

It's a simple message: buy good bread and use it well.

# 21

# FOR THE LOVE OF MENUS

When I was sixteen, I started to keep a book of menus, a school exercise book I'd carefully covered in wrapping paper. This was an odd obsession, because I didn't cook most of the menus I put together; I would've needed a restaurant to get through them all. The pleasure was in creating them, thinking long and hard about what dishes worked together.

I still have the book. Most of the meals are simple: cucumber salad with dill and soured cream, goulash, baked autumn fruit; crudités (the kind I'd had in France), *poulet bonne femme, galette aux pommes*. There aren't any dishes from some of the cuisines I now love – Middle Eastern or Vietnamese, for example – but there are a few old-fashioned, embarrassingly complicated menus I wouldn't dream of attempting these days: buckwheat blinis with warm melted butter, soured cream and smoked salmon, guinea fowl breasts in pastry with mushrooms *duxelles* and Madeira sauce, then Grand Marnier soufflé. I did actually cook this. Was I mad?

My parents didn't have dinner parties. They gave parties, though. These weren't formal, you were invited verbally ('Come on over. We're having a few people in'). They were about good craic, drinking Bushmills whiskey and Vat 69 and dancing to Nancy Sinatra. My mum prepared wonderful food, dishes that would be laid out, buffet-style, on the big dining table. She thought about what worked together. She was going to cookery classes (she was always going to cookery classes) and made dishes that were, for that time, exotic: braised pork with peppers and paprika, 'slaw with caraway seeds, an 'Austrian' coffee cake that was soaked in booze. Some of the recipes came from her classes, others from the Cordon Bleu partwork she was collecting (and which I pored over at night until my eyes hurt).

From these parties, as well as from the pages of Cordon Bleu, I got the idea that having people round to eat wasn't just about food, but about creating an event, an atmosphere.

I gave my first 'dinner party' soon after I started keeping my menu book. My school friends were bemused by the candlelit room (I'd gone over the top). 'Are we going to celebrate mass?' one asked. And they didn't quite get the pineapple water ice ('What is this?') but I continued, undaunted. I loved 'having people over' but, even more, I loved putting a menu together.

Years later, I discovered Alice Waters's *Chez Panisse Menu Cookbook*, a thrill for the menu fanatic. The book contains recipes, of course, but it's also an archive of menus served at Chez Panisse restaurant in Berkeley, California. The place was unusual, especially for that time, in that it offered only set menus. Set menus were and are common in France, but, when Alice started serving them in the 1970s, they were not the norm either in America or Britain. As Chez Panisse was run mostly by people who weren't trained chefs, it made sense to offer the same food to everyone – they couldn't have managed a big à la carte menu – and I was fascinated by the meals they'd put together. It wasn't restauranty, it was like the food a very good and thoughtful home cook would make.

When I moved to London in the mid-1980s, I soon learned that Clarke's restaurant – owned and run by Sally Clarke, who had worked at Chez Panisse – also offered set menus. I used to get on the Tube on a Monday night to go and see what Sally had planned for the week. I'd stand there, sometimes in the rain, writing down her menus in a notebook. I rarely ate at Clarke's (I was in my first job and it was expensive), but I felt as if I ate there all the time. Composing a menu is still my favourite bit of cooking.

I don't invite people round and then wonder what I'll cook, I come up with a menu and then consider who would like to eat it.

I get more questions about menus than about anything else. Friday nights and Saturday mornings bring endless phone calls and texts. Friends, preparing meals for Saturday night, have decided on a main course but don't know what to have for pudding (puddings are nearly always an afterthought), and everybody wants a 'quick' starter. 'Will these dishes work together?' is something I'm always being asked.

There are some practical 'rules' about menus, though they're open to being bent, even completely broken. Ideally, no more than two courses should be cooked at the last minute, otherwise you'll be stressed. (This rule can be dispensed with if you are one of those cooks who can deep-fry while making sparkling conversation with twelve people. I am not one of those cooks.) A meal shouldn't be too rich: cream should only appear in one course (though you can always have it with pudding). It's not ideal to repeat ingredients. In general, if I start with fish, it won't appear again (though I break this 'rule'). Consider colour, texture and temperature and – it almost goes without saying – eat seasonally.

Make sure your guests aren't going to be full by the end of the first course (the Australian restaurateur, Gay

Bilson, has written that the appetite should be piqued as you eat, rather than sated).

I love mezze and tapas – you get to taste so many different things – and I understand the modern desire for 'small plates', but I still cleave, mostly, to the notion of a meal that progresses from one course to the next, however recent, in historical terms, that idea is.

I often start meals with a salad, because it's such an 'appetite-opening' way to begin, but you don't need a 'starter' at all. You can always begin with things guests can pick at: radishes, charcuterie, olives. Radishes with quail's eggs and tapenade – or just with good bread, butter and salt – is my go-to opener. Then there are crudités. These are not the sorry flaccid raw-vegetables-plus-dip that you see in supermarkets, but the small array of vegetable salads – *carottes rapées, lentilles en salade*, leeks vinaigrette – that the French serve.

A main course doesn't have to be a hunk of protein with side dishes, it can be about the same size as the starter, and it doesn't have to be meat- or fish-based at all. Soup is hard to fit into any dinner (it's just too filling), but lunch can be built on it. I love a plain leaf salad; you can slot them into any meal. It was one of the things I came to appreciate on my first trip to France and became almost my favourite part of every meal; it was cleansing and refreshing and provided a kind of interlude. But the leaves have to be good, and good leaves don't come pre-washed in a bag. Buy proper lettuce in heads; depending on the variety it will keep in the fridge for days (especially curly endive, chicory and Baby Gems). Wash what you need, dry the leaves thoroughly and make a good vinaigrette, by which I mean taste it as you make it. There are agreed general proportions for vinaigrette, of course, but they will vary for each one you make, depending on the vinegar and the oil you are using, as well as the leaves you are dressing.

Puddings can be dropped in favour of cheese – and remember that one good cheese is better than four average pieces – a perfectly ripe bit of fruit, or a glass of dessert wine. I prefer fruit puddings, though sometimes I long for something chocolatey and slightly bitter. I love ices; you can fuse flavours in them. An ice can combine grapefruit and basil, chocolate and luscious sweet Pedro Ximénez, bourbon, maple syrup and apples.

You don't always have to serve bread, but it's important with mezze-type meals, as they generally contain dishes that need to be scooped up. If you're going to have bread, serve good stuff, and good butter or olive oil, too.

There is poetry in menus. They can transport you to the Breton coast, or to a Saturday night in Manhattan; they are short stories. The conjuring-up of place through food is very important to me. It's one of the reasons I cook. I think this is because I grew up in Northern Ireland.

I didn't go abroad until I was fifteen, when I travelled to France on my own, on an exchange trip. There were very few destinations you could fly to directly from Belfast; you generally had to go via London, which meant that travelling was expensive. If you wanted to go places, you had to do it in your head – via books – or by cooking the food of other countries. When I did start to travel, everywhere seemed very intense: Spain (raw light, heat, olive oil, the smell of tobacco) was very Spanish; New York really did have Walk/Don't Walk signs; Morocco felt almost biblical. I love travelling, but I'm quite timid. I feel difference very keenly. I notice everything and the sense of a place stays with me. Part of my cooking is about revisiting places, and even expressing feelings about particular places.

The term 'entertaining' makes me think of hostess trollies and instructions on how to plump up your cushions. I really don't do 'entertaining'. I just have friends round. Often, I serve dinner (or supper, or whatever you want to call it) in the midst of a mess, otherwise I wouldn't see friends at all. I'm happy to put a roasting tin on the table and ask someone else to carve (I am terrible at carving). I don't think you should kill yourself over dinner, but at the same time I do like all the stuff that goes with it: table linen, plates, old cutlery. I have spent a lifetime gathering this up and I like spending time on it, when I can.

Having people round to eat is about food... and yet it isn't. Meals, no matter how simple, are made better by small things: flowers, candles, a jug of water. They're also made bad by small things: salami served in the plastic packet in which it comes, poor bread. I don't like the suggestion – prevalent these days – that cooking is all about 'lifestyle'. I think it's about taking care of the small, seemingly unimportant things.

In a single moment, I realized how much other people care about these small things, too. At a restaurant in Italy (on my first trip there), the diners at the next table didn't have a fancy dessert, they just had a bowl of peaches and a bottle of cold Moscato. Everyone sliced their peach and dropped it into the wine. After a while, they drank the wine – now imbued with the flavour of the peach – and ate the peach slices, which now tasted of the wine. This was not a complicated dish, but it was a lovely way to end a meal – seasonal, straightforward, caring, even a little magical – and it illustrated an approach to food and cooking that I already understood but hadn't yet articulated. I've never forgotten this. More than a memory, those peaches became a symbol of what good food is all about.

## 22

# A GOOD BIRD

Chicken, in its many guises, has always been part of my life. Chicken Maryland, a big chunk of golden-skinned bird served with fried bananas and bacon, was what my siblings and I ordered when we went out to supper as kids. Sitting on modish chairs with scratchy seats, our feet barely touching the ground, we tackled plates of this in the local 'grillroom' (such things existed in the 1970s) with appetites that were bigger than our child-sized bellies. At home, roast chicken with parsley and onion stuffing – served with my mum's chips – was the meal that always provoked cheers. As teenagers, picnics weren't based on sandwiches, but on a whole cold roast chicken whose meat we would tear apart and stuff into soft white rolls. Chicken curry (the old-fashioned British kind made with curry paste, raisins and the remains of the roast) was the exotic accompaniment to Sunday night telly.

When I was taken to supper by a boy I really fancied – only to have him tell me that he was interested in my best friend – I was eating chicken (it was probably the only time in my life I didn't polish it off).

Chicken is the thing I sneak into the fridge to steal and the first dish I order when I arrive in Portugal (piri piri) or the States (fried). At the end of a filming day with Hugh Fearnley-Whittingstall (I was a TV producer before I was a food writer), we were finishing dinner when Hugh looked at the remains of the bird on my plate. It was hard to tell from the clean little bones what I had eaten, but Hugh knew. 'What did you do to that poussin?' he asked (with more than a little admiration). 'I stripped it to its bones,' I said. 'Just as I was taught.' This is down to my dad, who always pointed out the little morsels you hadn't managed to extricate from the carcass and was fond of all the tastiest bits: the oysters (those little plump cushions of meat on the underside), the crisp-tipped wings, the juicy thighs. In my family, we were instructed in the enjoyment of chicken.

And it appears to be dear – or at least a good buddy – to others, too. Fried chicken, chicken tikka masala, jerk chicken… many cultures cherish chicken dishes. It is also the meat most people – even those who aren't keen on meat – will eat. It's amenable, too, and I mean that in a good way. It's the basic outfit that you can dress down (for picky children) or dress up (on those occasions when you want to present a dish that prompts everyone to ask for the recipe). My efforts with it range from bashing strips of chicken breast, dipping them in egg and breadcrumbs and frying them (a favourite of my kids), to a golden roasted bird surrounded by glossy chestnuts and prunes. In between, I make chicken dishes from all over the world. There isn't a week goes by that I don't cook chicken at least once.

When 'foodies' complain about how 'tasteless' they find chicken, I'm really not sure what they're doing with it. If you have chicken in the fridge, a good meal is never far away.

# 23
# A BARREL OF CUKES

America seems to be two countries. Many regard the States as some kind of low-rent fast food outlet, the home of all we decry, such as fatty burgers and supersized buckets of cola. But this ignores the wider picture. Americans' concern for freshness, localness and seasonality, as expounded by chefs such as Alice Waters, the mother of Californian cuisine, has had a bigger effect on how we eat (and how chefs cook) than you might know, and many Americans take home-preserving very seriously indeed. They love their burgers and their salt beef sandwiches, and pickles and relishes are vital for these. They will wax lyrical about the sour fermented cukes they stole from the cloudy brine of a pickle barrel as kids. I have spent days travelling in New England, seduced by roadside stalls and farm shops into buying jars of bread-and-butter pickles, beach plum jelly and pickled dilly beans.

In Vermont, I've watched people boil apple juice to make cider syrup to bottle and 'put up', seen notices for community suppers with a menu of baked ham, baked potatoes and pickled pumpkin, and attended 'sugar on snow' parties to celebrate the maple syrup season, where the sweetness of the syrup is cut with bites of sour pickles. Make no mistake, American preserving isn't a folksy romantic notion: it is alive and well and increasing in popularity.

Native Americans practised some forms of preserving, most notably drying, then European settlers brought all sorts of domestic skills with them, especially pickling in brine and vinegar. Since then, waves of immigrants from Italy, Germany, Poland, Greece, China and Korea, plus Jews from all over Europe, have imported their own traditions.

At school, I loved the stories of Laura Ingalls Wilder and her *Little House in the Big Woods*. I was surprised, when I re-read them as an adult, that they had held my attention, because they are, in large part, accounts of the preparations undertaken to 'put up' food for the winter. The food that you preserved was crucial for getting through the cold months. In areas where heavy snow was the norm, you couldn't even leave the house. Families would have starved without food that had been pickled, bottled, dried, salted or smoked.

The Southern States don't have snowy winters, but preserving is a huge tradition there too, because of a different instinct: the desire not to squander food. Who could waste the peaches and corn, the tomatoes and melons? You can't even read books set in the American Deep South without wanting to cook: Southern literature is splattered with hunger and its cures. Sitting on a porch during one of Carson McCullers's 'green and crazy' summers, you would want to eat smiling wedges of watermelon and pickle the rind later.

Very few countries have ever had a leader capable of writing this: 'On a hot day in Virginia, I know nothing more comforting than a fine spiced pickle, brought up trout-like from the sparkling depths of the aromatic jar below the stairs of Aunt Sally's cellar.' That's Thomas Jefferson. Doesn't it make you want to fill your coolest, airiest cupboards with jars? It does me. Just find me a porch and get me a pitcher of lemonade. I have a load of peaches to stone.

# 24
# LEFTOVERS

As I was growing up, I learned the art of dove-tailing meals: always using up leftovers. This was not out of poverty, but because a philosophy of using every bit of an animal and not throwing out food prevailed. This is good for the household budget, but it's also a sane way to think about the world's resources. The word 'leftovers' does not sound great. The French, more charmingly, call them *les délicieux petits restes*. They have the right approach: leftovers can produce some of the most imaginative and delicious meals.

My favourite kind of cooking is not the showy-off sort, which takes days of planning and shopping, but the pottering, 'I-wonder-what's-in-the-fridge' kind. There's no grand plan: you just go where serendipity and improvisation take you. Monday, when there's a bit of weekend roast left, is the best day for this musing kind of approach. Chicken – if you can get your hands on it – is perfect (though we fight over cold roast chicken in our house). Fry the leftover nuggets with bacon, a couple of tablespoons of cream and a handful of frozen peas and you have a sauce for pasta. (Even half a cup of gravy, fried mushrooms and a dollop of cream are delicious on pasta.) You can toss shredded chicken with rice, strips of omelette and chilli to make a perfect hangover cure too.

Cold roast lamb, cooked nice and pink so that a bit more heat won't harm it, can form the basis of a Middle Eastern pilaf that will be just as enjoyable as yesterday's roast. If you have some preserved lemon to throw in, or a few dried apricots, so much the better. What of leftover veg? Potatoes are easy. Sauté slowly – maybe with some mushrooms – until the pan is covered with golden flakes, finish with garlic and parsley, and you have a dish that is perfect with duck or chicken.

And then there is stock. Get those bones into a pot. There is so much flavour still to be extracted, it is a shame to throw them away. It takes next to no effort and you can reduce the result by boiling, then freeze it in tubs. Soups and sauces are then yours for the making (and although it's great that you can now buy fresh stock, just look at its price; much better to make your own).

The art of using food up even goes as far as finding something to do with a bag of soft plums. They can easily be transformed into a pot of jam. You don't have to get out a preserving pan and go into full-scale production: it's very easy to make just one small pot and keep it in the fridge for eating on toast or with yogurt at breakfast.

For me, the path to contentment definitely wends its way past the stove, but it's always a good idea to go via the remains in the fridge.

# SOFT HERBS

We get so used to employing certain herbs in particular ways: a little mint sprig imparting an echo of itself to new potatoes; leaves of basil sweetening a plate of vine tomatoes; handfuls of chopped parsley giving a final celery-like freshness to a long-simmered chicken soup.

In fact, it's often impossible to smell these herbs without simultaneously smelling the dishes they so commonly infuse. Like a partner in a comfy marriage, we begin to see them only in a particular light, or even cease to notice them at all. Then, suddenly, you taste a new dish, from a different country, using the same old herb, and it's like being with a different person. Parsley – great coarsely chopped mounds of it – when mixed with slivers of onion and abundant lemon juice, is suddenly brash, effortlessly cutting through the spices of Middle Eastern lamb kofta. Mint finds herself being eaten by the handful with sheep's cheese and flatbread as a Persian appetizer. And basil, well she, dancing with her new partners, parsley and coriander, in a Georgian dish of fish with aubergines and pomegranates, is positively triumphant. 'Thought you'd keep me holed up in that little apartment in Genoa,' she seems to jeer, 'Well, I've got news for YOU!'

For Middle Eastern dishes, you can forget those pathetic little packs of greenery that pass for bunches of herbs in the supermarkets. In the Middle East, herbs aren't just used to perfume or embellish a dish; in many cases they *are* the dish and you have to buy them by the armful. Leaving a Middle Eastern greengrocer, your head swims with the citrusy aroma of your bouquet of coriander, or the cleansing scent of a bunch of mint that could see you through a year of mint sauce. It's enough to make you want to roll around in grassy meadows.

It took just one meal in a Persian restaurant for me to see these soft-leaved flavour bombs as players in their own right. The classic Iranian appetizer, *sabzi khordan*, was set on our table while we were still looking through the menu. It's nothing more than a bowl of fresh herbs, artlessly thrown together, a slab of feta-like sheep's cheese, some radishes, spring onions and sheets of warm flatbread. The herb bowl should contain a mixture of tarragon, basil, mint and costmary (which is quite like watercress), though I've been served flat leaf parsley and coriander as part of it, too. The idea is that you pick at this tangle, pulling the leaves of basil and tarragon from their stalks and eating them with the bread, radishes and cheese. The bowl stays on the table throughout the meal in case you want to chew a little mint with your skewered lamb or add a little parsley to your rice. Left this unadulterated, you taste the herbs as if for the first time. And yes, aniseedy tarragon works surprisingly well with sheep's cheese; mint, eaten leaf-by-leaf instead of just as a flavour in cooking water, zings across your palate; basil, away from its tomato partnership, suddenly tastes of cinnamon.

Iranians, along with other Middle Eastern cooks, use familiar herbs in ways that, to Northern European and American sensibilities, are quite unexpected. Take dill: the greenish-blue fronds, which you associate with cold northern climes, whose caraway scent flavours Scandinavian cured salmon and Russian borscht. Dill's as big in Iran as it is in Sweden and there's so much of it in Persian broad bean pilaf that you have trouble seeing the rice. Dill also goes into braised spinach, soups and herb-laden stews. The Greeks and Turks love dill too, adding it to rice and bulgur pilafs, or mixing it with ground lamb for kofta and with eggs and feta for stuffing filo pies. Further east, in Georgia, dill's stirred, at the last minute, into plum sauce to serve with fried chicken and sour cherry pilaf to serve with lamb. Feta, broad beans, lamb and tart red fruits... dill's great with them all. So for dill there is definitely life beyond gravlax.

And for parsley there is life beyond chicken soup, because nobody honours parsley like the Lebanese. There, as throughout the Med, parsley is the flat leaved variety, not the curly type, and it's treated as a salad leaf as well as a flavouring. The ubiquitous tabbouleh is such a parsley-fest it's difficult to divine that tomato and bulgur wheat lurk there too. Parsley is also layered with tomatoes, warm rags of pitta bread and cucumber to make the Lebanese salad, fattoush, while the herb finds its way into most of the marinades that imbue meat destined for the Lebanese grill.

In North Africa, huge handfuls of chopped parsley are mixed with black olives, finely chopped red onion, slivers of preserved lemon and olive oil to make an aggressive salad, and parsley's one of the main ingredients in the Moroccan herb and spice relish, chermoula. Blithely sunbathing with coriander, cumin, chilli and cinnamon, it's hard to believe that parsley ever soothes us in the creamy embrace of a parsley sauce. But a whole new side of parsley's personality comes to the fore when it co-stars with the eastern flavour of coriander. Try adding coriander and parsley together, instead of coriander on its own, to Moroccan tajines of chicken and pickled lemons, or to lamb and apricots, to see just how out of the ordinary parsley can be.

Coriander's a funny one. The most widely used herb in the world – in India, South-East Asia, South America and the Middle East – people either love it or loathe it. It's been described as 'fetid' and 'sweaty' and its ancient Greek name, *koris*, means 'bed bug'... though unless you spend your time sniffing mattresses in insalubrious places, I'm not sure how you'd be familiar with their scent. You don't come across coriander in European Mediterranean dishes, except in Portuguese cooking. There they stir coriander into rice, add it to broad beans with bacon, scatter it over fried potatoes and put it in the salad bowl.

But in the Middle East they use it with total abandon, perhaps because its pungent citrus flavour cries out for chilli, lemon and cumin. Coriander can take centre stage, puréed with spices, lemon, garlic and oil to make a sauce, or thrown into a bowl for an eastern-tasting salad. But it can also play something of the role that lemon takes, that of flavour-enhancer. Coriander completes a spicy lentil stew, bringing out something that even lemon can't; it pulls together the disparate elements in an Egyptian stuffing of walnuts, pomegranates and garlic; it intensifies the fruitiness of a Georgian blackberry sauce. There are so many flavours with which it works well – cumin, garlic, lemon and lime, ginger, chilli, saffron and sour red fruits – that coriander can be a good mate as well as the leader of the pack. I like it for that.

Mint, too, can insinuate or look you straight in the eye. Away from the confines of a bowl of English peas, she's pretty determined to jettison the subtle approach and who can blame her? She has sweetness as well as cleanness; there are tones of cinnamon, dill and lemon alongside the mint.

Persians put mint in lamb and rhubarb stew; Sicilians add it to tomato salad and tomato sauce, or layer it with grilled vegetables bathed in a sweet-sour vinaigrette; Andalusians cook it with oranges and duck. All over the Middle East, whole mint leaves are thrown into salads, mixed into ground lamb, mashed with feta and stirred into pilafs. And what about yogurt, garlic and mint? That divine trinity is present at almost every Middle Eastern meal I serve. Even the dried stuff is used in the Middle East, and, though I find it a bit musty, a swirl of what they call 'burnt mint' (dried mint fried in butter or oil) looks and tastes good in wintry soups and bowls of yogurt and cucumber.

Fresh, though, mint is never hard to find; it grows so easily that you have trouble finding uses for it. The Moroccans have the perfect solution: mint tea. It's not just that it tastes great, it's that it does great things to your head: clearing, freshening and soothing all at the same time, leaving you alert but not hyper. No wonder Pliny suggested students should wear a wreath of mint to 'exhilarate their minds'. Put some sugar and a handful of spearmint leaves in a pot, cover with boiling water and leave to infuse for five minutes. Pour the tea from a height to aerate and disperse the perfume and embrace a drink that will make you feel like you've been running in a forest.

Apart from the Persian herb bowl, basil isn't really used in the Middle East. The Greeks regard it as sacred – there you're more likely to see it on the church altar than in the kitchen – and the Moroccans keep it in their gardens to ward off insects; a tribute, I suppose, to its power. But of all these herbs, basil has the greatest capacity to surprise. Tear a leaf in half and smell it. Now taste it. It's full of spices: pepper, cinnamon and sweet, sweet cloves, making it a candidate for experimentation.

I've used basil with coriander and parsley (a tastebud-dazzling combination) in Georgian plum sauce and in lamb or chicken braises heavy with pomegranates or sour cherries. In fact, it's a really good fruit herb. Lemon and basil is quite an obvious pairing, but try basil too in ice creams or sorbets made with apples, plums, raspberries, mangoes or pineapples. And put it in the poaching liquid for peaches or nectarines.

As with all these herbs, basil's oils are volatile, so add them to cooked dishes a few minutes before serving. And, just to settle an old culinary conundrum, you should tear basil instead of cutting it if you don't want the edges to go brown. According to the culinary scientist, Harold McGee, tearing separates the leaves along its cell walls; cutting slices through them. Now you know.

# 26

# SUMMER'S END

It's hard to know whether to feel sad or excited as summer slides into autumn, and it's difficult to pinpoint exactly when summer's gone. Autumn advances in small steps. We teeter between ease and anticipation. It can still be warm and the stalls in front of the greengrocer's shop display an almost embarrassing abundance as the seasons collide. Can I really have figs, late raspberries and corn?

I think of America, of all those farm stands where the first pumpkins try to nudge the corn out of the way. Back in my kitchen, I make fruit compotes and American desserts. Those homely fruit-rich slumps and grunts and buckles are perfect at this time of year. They nod to the season to come, as well as to the one that's departing.

And then there's the last of the corn. I'm stupidly romantic about corn. For years, I had a London Transport poster from the 1920s on my bedroom wall. It was called

'Flowers o' the Corn' and showed a golden world of poppies and cornflowers growing among corn and grasses. The line at the bottom of the poster read: 'How Near the Corn Grows'. I assume these posters were designed to make you yearn to take a train to the English countryside, but this particular picture made me want to go to the States. I only realized recently that I had always misread the last line, transposing the letters of the first two words. 'Now hear the corn grow,' I used to whisper when I looked at the image. I daydreamed about lying in a field in the Midwest, ears of corn towering above me, concentrating on the sound as the corn reached towards the sun.

American friends tell me – winking – that you can lie in a cornfield and hear the rustle. As it grows, a corn stalk expands, stretching and crackling. In nature, this happens slowly, but scientists have recorded it and speeded it up. If you want, you can find recordings online. Hear the corn grow.

Goodbye to corn, but hello to smoked food and roasts. If it's warm enough, enjoy summer's last stand in the garden.

27

# ASH KEYS AND MANGOES ON THE ROOF

'High tea', a very British kind of meal, was what I used to have at my great-grandmother's house on a Sunday. It consisted of cold cuts, a loaf of white bread, tomatoes, a big cool pat of butter, hard-boiled eggs, soft-leaved lettuce and a whole assortment of jars. Every jar had its own spoon and there was a special pickle fork, too. The British love their jars of pickles and chutneys. The basics of a meal – the meat, or a pie – may be solid and seemingly unexciting, but we are very good at 'tracklements', the bits that are served on the side. The contents of these jars are an illustration of our history, and also our magpie tendencies to steal what we have fallen in love with from other cultures.

There has been an explosion in the range of 'hand-crafted' pickles and chutneys and an increasing number of good artisan producers. We've come a long way since there was just Sharwood's mango chutney to go with our Vesta curry, and Branston for cheese and pickle sandwiches. But there was a whole world of chutneys and pickles before the commercial varieties took off. The larders of 16th- and 17th-century England would have been wondrous places to explore. We have pickled since the Roman invasion, but it became more popular in Elizabethan times, partly because a greater range of fruit and vegetables became available and partly because Elizabethans were very concerned with how their food looked. They used delicate pickles, even pickled flowers – cowslips, violets and gilly flowers – to decorate salads. In fact, almost anything was a potential pickle. Writers such as Gervase Markham, Robert May and John Evelyn describe pickles made from ash keys and broom buds as well as lettuce and cucumber.

Something approaching a mania for 'a bit on the side' took hold when unusual pickles and chutneys from the East India Company began to arrive in Britain in the late 17th century ('chutney' comes from the Hindustani word *chatni*, meaning a strong, sweet relish). British cooks tried to imitate Chinese and Malayan 'catsup', made from fermented fish, by making mushroom, anchovy and walnut catsups, and they used melons, cucumber and peaches to make mock mango pickle. The first recipe for piccalilli (not as British as you think) actually appeared in 1694 with the title 'To pickle lila, an Indian pickle'.

Eliza Acton, in *Modern Cookery for Private Families*, published in 1845, has a short section on chutneys and pickles, but writes very clear instructions, suggesting that she made them often. She gives recipes for eastern 'chatneys', meant to be eaten with curries and cold cuts, others which hark back to the Elizabethan age (pickled nasturtiums), and plenty of pickled fruits (not surprising as they are excellent with cheeses and raised pies).

There was a whole range of commercially made pickles and chutneys in the Victorian era, all heavily flavoured with the spices the English had come to love. Chutneys with glorious names like Major Grey and Bengal Club echoed the days of the Raj, days of tennis parties, pink gimlets and blazing hot sun. Our British versions were good in their own right, but much sweeter, and nothing like as vibrant – in colour or taste – as the Indian originals that had inspired them.

In India, pickles and chutneys have a more central role in the meal, and in life. 'In India, pickles are power,' says Roopa Gulati. Roopa, brought up in India and Cumbria, was shocked, when she began married life in Delhi, to find just how much a woman's sense of self-worth is bound up with her pickle- and chutney-making skills. 'Food is a weapon there, as well as a nurturing tool. Women are so possessive of their pickling recipes and methods that they don't hand them to their daughters, that way the recipes would pass into another family. They give them to their daughters-in-law, so that they stay close to home.' Roopa's mother-in-law kept such a close eye on her pickles that she stored them in her bedroom. 'Even the children's nanny wouldn't share her recipes!' Roopa whispers. 'I used to say her mango chutney was the best I'd ever tasted and asked what was in it. She would just smile and say, "Oh, this and that." In all the years she lived with us, she got up early to prepare her chutneys, so she could do it in private.'

The relish tray is as important in an Indian household as the main meal. They're far more than just condiments. Some, especially fresh chutneys, can be eaten in large quantities, as if they were salads, and deciding which recipes to make fresh every day is a major preoccupation. Small wonder, as the range of pickles and chutneys in India is vast. There are hot pickles, sour pickles, oily pickles and 'water pickles', which are briny. Then there are chutneys. Chutneys are sweeter than pickles, and much less chunky. Many chutneys are made to be eaten fresh, others are designed to last (well-stored) for years, ageing and mellowing like good wine. Sweetness is added to chutneys in the form of jaggery, while sourness comes from tamarind and limes as well as from vinegar.

Oil pickles – *achar* – are a particularly popular type of pickle that is relatively unknown in Britain outside Indian families. In India, mustard oil, untoasted sesame oil and vegetable oil are used for these. The pickles must always be protected under a good layer of oil and their success depends on a long marination time.

Chutneys and pickles are not used with rich or delicate foods, such as creamy kormas, but with plain rice pilaus, dals and breads. Dharamjit Singh, in the 1970 Penguin Book *Indian Cookery*, suggests eating plain rice and vegetables with raita and up to a dozen pickles and chutneys, in order to experience them properly.

Chutney- and pickle-making is something that groups of women do together, especially family groups. 'In rural areas in particular you know when pickles are being made,' says Roopa. 'You can see ingredients drying outside. Mangoes on the rooftops.' This is because many chutneys and pickles are 'cooked' in the heat of the sun. 'To make lime pickle, we would put a cross in the top of each fruit, then stuff them with chilli, spices and salt, put them in pots covered with cheesecloth and leave them on the roof. Every day they had to be stirred with a wooden spoon. After two weeks in the sun, the limes would be soft and salty. When I was growing up in Cumbria we did the same thing, but put them beside the fire to "cook".'

Chutneys and pickles are vibrant and 'living', their piquancy mellowing into something rounded. And their flavours are deep. It helps you understand why Indians see pickles and chutneys as more than just accompaniments...

... And why this little scrap of Indian verse from the days of the Raj is so apt: 'All things chicken'y and mutton'y taste better far when served with chut-a-ney.'

## 28

# THE COLOUR PURPLE

For a bit of dark glamour in the cold months, I turn to plums and sour little black damsons. The misty bloom of their skins, the spectrum of colours they encompass – purple, black, dark blue, amber and russet – and the texture of the skins, somewhere between velvet and suede, echo the softer fabrics we begin to wear once September arrives. I'm drawn to their rich, purply blotches of colour: study them through half-closed eyes and it looks as though they've been drawn in smudgy pastels.

Of course, plums are summer as well as autumn fruits: you see the first of them in July. But the classic summer fruits, such as tart, bright raspberries and redcurrants, put a spring in your step and make you think of blue skies; plums make me want to close the front door and put the oven on.

I'm a sucker for baked and poached fruits and plums take to this treatment brilliantly. Poach or bake them in red wine with sugar or honey, with herbs such as thyme, fennel, bay and rosemary, or spices such as cinnamon, ginger and cardamom... each combination will give different results. Scoop the fruits out of the cooking liquid when they are just tender, reduce the juice, leave it to cool and thicken, then pour it back over the fruit and chill: simple and delicious.

Plums are one of the most useful fruits in the autumn kitchen. The Austrians put them into tarts, pastry slices, cakes and dumplings and the Hungarians, Poles and Russians can't get enough of them either, making them into plum brandy and vodka, or using them in sauces to eat with game, grilled chicken and lamb kebabs.

But plums can be a lottery. They often look as if they'll be full of sweet-sour purple juice, but taste of nothing. Luckily, even a poor plum responds well to heat and sugar, so it's poaching or roasting for them. Victorias, the plums we tend to see most in the shops, are the Golden Delicious of the plum world: bland, without the requisite touch of sharpness that makes for a really good plum. But I still use them, enhanced with lemon juice, when they are cheap and abundant. Better are the more marginal varieties of plum, such as Warwickshire Drooper, Kirke's Blue and Purple Pershore. Farmers' markets and farm shops are the places to look for such fruit. Gages are generally considered to have the best flavour of all. The greengage, or Reine-Claude as it is known in France, is available from late August and is perfect for French-style open tarts, or just eating out of your hand. Gages are sweeter and more delicate than most plums and you shouldn't miss the chance to eat a Coe's Golden Drop, of which the epicure Edward Bunyard wrote, in *The Anatomy of Dessert*: '... the skin is rather tough, but between this and the stone floats an ineffable nectar'. I'm very influenced by colour, though; I want blood-red juices staining my crumbles, so it's dark plums that I will always choose for cooking.

Damsons – small, dark oval plums – are the tartest of all autumn fruits. Their deep crimson colour is so spectacular that it's no wonder they were used as a dye in the past. Don't think about eating them raw: they need both sugar and cooking. And forget about trying to stone them; the pit is so tightly embedded that it won't budge. For jam and chutney – damsons are great for these, producing big, dark, fruity jarfuls – remove the stones after cooking, by pushing the fruit through a sieve. Damsons also make great crumbles, pies and cobblers: their sourness really cuts through pastry. For these, I leave it to diners to pick out the stones.

You have to be quick to get hold of damsons, mind you, and it's best to know someone with a tree. They're picked from the end of August for about eight weeks. Supermarkets and greengrocers largely seem to ignore them, but then there is something special about a fruit that takes effort to track down. It seems appropriate to make old-fashioned country dishes with them. Damson cheese – a dark, firm jelly made from boiling and reducing damson flesh with sugar – is a better foil for lamb than redcurrant jelly and superb with strong cheeses. The deep, fruity flavour will keep you going through the winter months.

Sadly, prunes still suffer from being the subject of schoolboy giggles, because of their laxative qualities. It's an ingredient I hesitate to cook for people I don't know well, in case they associate prunes with nannies, fagging and Latin conjugations, but other Europeans love them. Again, it's the cooks of South-West France – where the fruit was traditionally shipped through the river port of Agen (hence the name for their prunes, *pruneaux d'Agen*) – who can teach us how to use them: rabbit, pork and duck legs are braised with prunes, spiced prunes are served with pork and rabbit terrines, while their dessert table boasts prune clafoutis, prune tart and prune-and-Armagnac ice cream.

Why don't we honour this dark fruit in such a way? The Danes love them too, stuffed into loin of pork or pickled and eaten with open sandwiches, while the

Russians and the Poles both eat them in pork dishes and in festive compotes, poached along with dried figs. I'm not convinced that the best prunes are from Agen, despite their reputation. There are very good Californian prunes, and I select them according to how I want to cook them. *Mi-cuit*, the semi-dried ones, don't have the shelf life of fully dried prunes, but are delicious for snacks, make great devils-on-horseback and are good in any dish in which they won't be cooked for long. For compotes or pickling, I buy the properly dried ones, which need soaking. The prunes to be careful of, delicious though they may be, are those in between fully dried and *mi-cuit*: they can catch you unawares by falling apart completely when cooked. You want your prunes to have a bit of body.

The prune's flavour bears little relation to that of the plum. A fresh plum is tart and juicy, while the dried version is rich, almost chocolatey. Apart from pairing them with rabbit – my favourite combination – prunes are brilliant standbys for making easy puddings. They keep for ages in their sealed packets, ready to be whipped out in an emergency and poached in wine or Earl Grey tea and sugar, soaked in Cognac or Armagnac and eaten with ice cream, or stuffed, Russian-style, with a walnut, before being doused in whipped cream. Stephanie Alexander, in her beautiful book *Cooking and Travelling in South-West France*, writes about prunes she was offered in place of dessert. They had been stoned, stuffed with marzipan and half a walnut, dipped in dark chocolate, and, once set, individually wrapped in deep-blue tissue paper. With a bitter espresso, I can't think of a better way to end a wintry meal.

# 29

# *TU VEUX UN APÉRITIF?*

The words *Tu veux un apéritif*? can be as heart-warming as *je t'aime* and as uplifting as the sound of a cork being pulled from a bottle. They make you feel simultaneously cherished and excited. An apéritif signals relaxation, and, often, a luxurious preamble to a good meal, though the *apéro* can be an occasion in itself, just half an hour's drinking with friends.

The habit of the apéritif is one of the most civilizing customs the French have given us, a simple pleasure that makes a small but significant difference to everyday life. And it crosses all classes. While madame is serving kirs on her vine-covered terrace, the local builders, sweat-smeared and dusty, will be knocking back glasses of milky pastis. The custom exists in other countries too, of course, but we got it from the French, that's why we use their word for it.

The first apéritif I tasted (in France when I was fifteen and totally unaccustomed to alcohol) was Pineau des Charentes, a fortified wine made from Cognac. That is commercially produced, but, at subsequent meals, glasses of homemade *vin d'orange* or kirs with homemade *vin de pêche* were served. These *vins maisons*, or *boissons de ménage*, were lovingly made by *tante* so-and-so or *mamie* (granny) in their kitchens. The food that accompanied them was always simple: slices of saucisson, olives or salted almonds, croûtes spread with goat's cheese, radishes with butter and salt, hard-boiled eggs with tapenade or a small spread of crudités. The apéritifs broke the ice and oiled conversation about the important things in life (wine, politics and infidelities), and could, if they were served with enough little titbits, act as an easy starter.

The apéritif was originally seen as something therapeutic, even medicinal. As far back as the Middle Ages, alcoholic drinks flavoured with herbs or spices were thought to be health-giving, and in the 19th century they started to be produced commercially.

If you want to buy your apéritif there are plenty of them, but you can make your own *vins maisons*. Some, such as *vin d'orange*, can be drunk straight, but others are used as mixers to produce drinks that are less well known outside France. Mix your homemade *crème de cassis* with dry cider to make a kir Breton, or add Champagne to

Breton sloe liqueur. A Parisian martini is made with gin, dry vermouth and *crème de cassis*. You can make *crème de framboises* – with raspberries instead of blackcurrants – and mix it with wine to produce a communard. In some areas, crème de cassis is mixed with red wine – producing a wintry kind of kir, a cardinal – and in Provence, fragrant *vin de pêche* is mixed with rosé.

Most *vins maisons* are the result of steeping fruit (sometimes leaves, herbs, spices or nuts) in eau de vie, but there are also ratafias. These are made in the same way, but use brandy. Once you've made a batch of either type, you'll get the bug, and can make a host of different drinks from summer and autumn fruits. There are drinks you can make for the end of the meal too, drunk as a digestif. But that's a whole other delicious story...

# HIBISCUS AND BLISTERED COBS

The Aeroméxico plane is being buffeted as if it was a toy, the windows illuminated every so often by lightning. '*Padre nuestro que estás en los cielos*,' the woman behind me prays in whispers. I feel guilty that my dominant emotion is exhilaration. Thirty minutes later I'm running across the tarmac, as my clothes get drenched by dark rain. My carry-on luggage – a cardboard box that houses a gaudy papier-mâché candelabra in the shape of a tree, tendrils of mad flowers clutching its trunk, wise owls sitting on its branches (bought because it reflected what I saw around me: vivid colours, a crazy kind of magic and a quiet sagacity in the people) – is so wet it's falling apart. At 1am, I swing through the doors of my hotel in Mérida to find a band playing 'La Bamba' and a bar serving *antojitos* (little snacks) of prawn fritters, chilli peanuts and pickled broad beans. There's a mezcal menu taped to the wall.

I'm suddenly so happy, it's as if I'd drunk my way through the list. Mexico, I think... it's a hip-swinging toe-tapping head rush.

This was my first trip to the country, defiantly undertaken after being dumped by my boyfriend. It's a good place to mend a broken heart.

I knew nothing about Mexican cooking – though I expected guacamole – and wasn't prepared for the extremes or the intricacies of the food. Some plates were citrus-fresh and simple: there was ceviche, slivers of pearlescent fish, their edges opaque from being 'cooked' in lime juice, served with raw onion, chilli and avocado. Other dishes were deep and layered: moles, the sauces for which Mexico is famous, slow braises, meat cooked in pits. You could see the colours – and the emotions – of Mexico's most famous painters, Diego Rivera and Frida Kahlo, in the food on your table.

When I got to Oaxaca, a beautiful city three hundred miles from the capital, I wanted my own kitchen, there was just so much to experiment with. The market sold fruits I'd never seen, a drink made from fermented pineapple, thousands of leathery chillies and baskets of spiced dried grasshoppers. In the middle of it all there was a vendor clutching a bunch of iridescent balloons. They shimmered. I wondered if this was what was meant by magical realism. If the balloon vendor had started to float heavenwards, I wouldn't have been surprised. I forgot all about the boyfriend.

To me, the great complex cuisines had been French and Chinese, but now I came to think that you couldn't call yourself a cook if you hadn't mastered Mexican sauces, their flavours built slowly and gradually. The dried chillies weren't about heat, but tone. They make you think of wood, tobacco, ripe autumnal fruit, chocolate – and provide the cook with a vast array of notes. I came to crave the sweet vanilla aroma of corn, the scent I most associate with Mexico.

For years after this trip, every time I drank a cold beer I would simultaneously smell the blistered cobs sold on street carts and the corn boiled with lime and ground to make *masa harina* (the body and soul of tortillas).

Mexicans are modest, they've never shouted about their food, but high-profile Mexican chefs are now demolishing the idea that their country's cuisine is merely avocados and tortilla chips. It's also about crimson hibiscus flowers, Mexican oregano, roses, cinnamon and allspice. And corn and beer, lime and tomatillos and the smoky chipotles that fixed my heart that summer.

# 31
# FROM THE HEARTH

I'm not one of those purist cooks who believe that you have to make everything yourself. I have never crafted my own sausages, dried my own fruit or brewed vinegar from the dregs of my guests' leftover wine.

Cooking should be about pleasure, not exhaustion, and there are some great food producers whose experience and skill you can never hope to better. But some foods are worth making yourself, either because you can't get a good commercial version, or because of the thrill of doing it, and because the results far outweigh the effort.

So it is with flatbreads. If you don't have a decent Turkish bakery at the end of your road (and most of us don't), or you'd like to take something out of your oven which is so earthy and basic that it feels like the first food ever cooked, then listen.

Flatbreads are everywhere. Fluffy naans and duvet-like focaccias, crisp-edged pizzas, pockets of pitta and crêpe-like tortillas. They're really user-friendly foods: great dippers, scooper-uppers, wrappers and bases for other ingredients. But most of the flatbreads we eat are processed and, frankly, they're not much cop. As far as supermarket pitta is concerned, you'd be better off eating cardboard.

Yet bread is the mainstay of the Middle Eastern meal, honoured by being the focus of the beggar's cry, 'Give me bread in the name of Allah!' In many Arab countries, it is picked up and cleaned if it falls on the ground. Loaves and sheets of bread are considered so special that people take considerable time buying them, or are immensely proud of their skill if they make them. They believe every bit of bread is unique. As Elias Canetti writes in *The Voices of Marrakesh*: 'In the evenings, after dark, I went to that part of the Djema el Fna where the women sold bread. They squatted on the ground in a long line... From time to time each would pick up a loaf of bread in her right hand, toss it a little way into the air, catch it again, tilt it to and fro a few times as if weighing it, give it a couple of audible pats, and then, these caresses completed, put it back on top of the other loaves. In this way the loaf itself, its freshness and weight and smell, as it were, offered themselves for sale.'

I yearn for bread like this: earthy, chewy dough to dip in the juices of a tajine, scoop up mezze or wrap around a chunk of spiced grilled meat. I want the pitta breads you get in Lebanese restaurants, hot from the oven, soft and cloud-light, puffed up like a genie's slippers. And I want sheets of Iranian *lavash* and *taftoon*, oatmeal-coloured and flecked with charring; looking like ancient bits of papyrus or huge pieces of plaster from some crumbling building, they demand to be torn, forcing you back to the world of their birth.

When I started to experiment and talk to cooks and bakers, I found that the flatbread world was even bigger than I had supposed. Despite their name, flatbreads are not always flat; they can, like focaccia, be quite deep and soft, or they can be as thin as a crêpe. Some flatbreads include yeast or bicarbonate of soda to help them rise; others have no raising agent at all. Funnily enough, some of the thinnest flatbreads are actually leavened, the effect experienced in the softly textured, pliable nature of the bread rather than in its height.

Some flatbreads are baked in the oven, others are fried and others still are cooked on a griddle or a terracotta stone. Presumably somebody arrived at the idea by leaving a porridge of pounded grain and water to dry out, or by accidentally baking a slab of the porridge on a hot stone, and flatbread was born. We know that the Egyptians called 'bread-eaters' by their neighbours in the ancient world, made flatbreads. The ingredients and methods are still very much the same now as they were then. Like all breads, flatbreads are simple. They are made of flour, water, salt and perhaps leavening. But flatbreads are much quicker to cook than big loaves, so they use less fuel. And their shape lends itself to being used as both plate and eating utensil, so you don't need anything else to complete your meal. For these reasons, flatbreads have always been the cheapest and most practical choice for peasants and nomadic people.

Italian focaccia was around well before ovens appeared on the scene. The dough was simply slapped on to a stone slab, flattened and covered with embers. Some Moroccan breads are cooked in a hole under the hot desert sands, while Iranians still make 'pebble bread', a lovely bubbly-textured bread that is cooked on, and indented by, small hot round stones. Other flatbreads are baked in ovens whose shape and design hasn't changed for centuries, such as the *tonir*, used to make *taftoon*. *Tonirs* are exactly the same as Indian tandoor ovens: barrel-shaped, open at the top and heated at the base by coal, wood or gas (or camel dung, if it's handy). In Iran, bakers use a special pillow to slap the round of dough on to the hot oven walls, where it cooks in minutes.

If you're not pressed for time, it's a pleasure to cook any bread. The dough feels lovely in your hands, like the most yielding pillow, and, when kneaded, as soft and smooth as a baby's cheek. But making flatbreads gives added pleasure, because they are such old foods. It's like cooking pieces of history. Perhaps this is why we baulk at making them ourselves. We suspect they can only be cooked in the alleys of Cairo, Fez or Istanbul, kneaded by men and women whose understanding of the mystique of bread has been absorbed from birth. It's true that these practitioners are brilliant at their craft, but it's a long way to go for a piece of pitta, and you can easily learn to turn out a passable imitation.

The main disadvantage of cooking these breads at home is that domestic ovens never get as hot as professional or wood-fired ovens. But if you put a baking sheet or pizza stone into a hot oven a good thirty minutes before you intend to cook flatbread, you can make a pretty good job of replicating those searing hot surfaces. Some flatbreads also adapt well to being cooked on a hot griddle, so you can try different methods and see which you prefer.

There are a few things that I've tripped up on in my bread-making history. Though flatbreads don't rise as much as regular loaves, the same rules apply. Make sure that the yeast is active, by leaving it to froth before adding it to the other ingredients. Too much salt, fat or sugar will inhibit the yeast's ability to work, or even kill it entirely, so don't add any more of these than indicated in the recipe. It's difficult to be precise about the amount of water you need in any bread, as this depends on the age of the flour and even on how humid the weather is, so add enough water to just bring your dough together, then add any more only a tablespoonful at a time. (You don't want to end up adding extra flour to save a soggy dough, as this will upset the balance of yeast to flour.)

If you're kneading by hand, there's no shortcut; you've got to develop the gluten in the flour so that it can stretch and hold, trapping the air you're incorporating and the carbon dioxide that makes the bread rise. You'll need to work at your dough for about fifteen minutes, until it is smooth and elastic and bounces back when you prod it with your finger. If you use a food mixer fitted with a dough hook to knead your bread, don't over work it – about seven minutes is fine – or the strands of gluten can become overextended and break.

When I'm too lazy to use even the dough hook, I make really quick unyeasted flatbreads, sometimes as substitutes for their more time-consuming relations. *Piadina* is an Italian flatbread from Emilia-Romagna that you often see wrapped around salami or prosciutto on bar counters. There's no rising time with *piadina*, so you can make it in a jiffy. You still get the salty, charred taste of pizza, though with a different texture, and I use *piadina* in much the same way, even though it's more often used as a wrap in its homeland. I also serve *piadina* instead of *khobz*, especially if I'm short of time. It feels good to have something warm and doughy on the table in less time than it takes to cook a pan of pasta.

*Socca*, made from a chickpea flour batter, could barely be called a bread at all, since it requires no rising or kneading and isn't doughy; it's really more like a thick crêpe. Though *socca*'s cooked in huge shallow pans in its native Nice, it works well as smaller individual cakes, making a really nutty-tasting base for strong-flavoured foods. And it takes about ten minutes to make.

The great thing about all these flatbreads is just how much you can do with them. Top a round of *piadina* with sausage and roast peppers, or grilled radicchio and smoked mozzarella, or a simple salad of tomato and basil moistened with enough olive oil to soak into the dough. Make your own kind of eastern garlic bread by brushing rounds of *khobz* with za'atar – a paste of thyme, sesame seeds, sumac and garlic mixed with olive oil – before you bake it, pricking it with a fork to ensure it doesn't balloon. Try *socca* with other Provençal flavours: anchoïade or tapenade, goat's cheese, red mullet, or sautéed squid with garlic. You'll also find that *socca* goes well with anything flavoured with cumin or coriander, maybe not surprisingly, since chickpea flour is used in Indian cooking.

And those wonderful Middle Eastern pocket breads, such as pitta, serve as pouches for so many things. Stuff them with houmous, grilled peppers or aubergines, spiced chicken or lamb, feta, olives, cucumbers and coriander leaves, yogurt and pickled chillies... where do I end?

There is no end. Flatbreads have been around for millennia and they'll be here for a long time to come. They're the most basic, usable, easy-to-make example of the staff of life.

# 32

# JAPANESE LESSONS

For me, discovering Japanese food was like being a reasonably good painter who suddenly finds a whole school of artists whose work is breathtaking. I had never looked beyond sushi when I won a haiku competition, the prize for which was a meal in a Michelin-starred Japanese restaurant in London. Going to Umu was like unlocking a secret. First, I literally couldn't find the way in. There didn't appear to be a door, though I knew I had the right address. I had to stand on the other side of the street and watch to see how other diners entered. One eventually came along, waved his hand over a sunken panel and the door opened. It was prophetic.

Umu is expensive but not glitzy. It is serene. The Japanese food experts I was with did the ordering… and it was a revelation. Each dish, served on plates and bowls of various textures, had a kind of quiet perfection, a completeness. There were expensive 'wow' dishes such as wagyu beef (which redefines the term 'melting') and a trembling custard of crab and ginger, but the dish I loved was the most simple: dashi, Japanese stock, with tofu that the chef had made himself. The tofu was like silk; the dashi like a liquid that had washed over seashells. As this meal went on, I became more and more happy. The best thing I get from my time in the kitchen is a gentle joy that things work, that dishes balance, come out harmoniously. But my cooking has big flavours and bright colours. Here was food that was quiet, that you approached in a micro eating style: you homed in on each texture, each colour – the tingle of a shiso leaf, the heat of a dab of wasabi. Appropriately, it was like eating a series of haiku.

You might think this was because I was in a Michelin-starred restaurant, but, some months later, I dined with – and took cooking instruction from – a Japanese food photographer called Yuki Sugiura. It was a drab day, filled with pewter-coloured drizzle. Yuki is not quiet and Zen-like – she is warm and excitable – yet her flat had the same peace as the restaurant. There was a big jug of rosehips on the table and the place was uncluttered. I sat down to another meal where texture, colour, taste and balance were key. There was freshly made dashi, an octopus salad with rice vinegar, carrots with a black sesame paste that Yuki had energetically pounded in a *suribachi* (a Japanese mortar), crunchy sweet-pickled lotus root, a wooden drum of warm rice. The incredible thing, though, was the cooked chrysanthemums. They are a much-loved seasonal treat in Japan, so I sat on a rainy day in South London at a table redolent with the flavours, textures and colours of a Japanese autumn.

In its use of vegetables and fish, it's a very healthy cuisine. And there is something in Japanese cooking that you can apply in your kitchen no matter what you're making; it's a particular psychological approach to food. There is an intense appreciation of detail. One of the tenets of Japanese cooking is to try to have balance across a meal. The ideal is to have five colours within one meal. Texture is vital and that doesn't just come from the foods themselves, but from the way they are cooked. Again, the Japanese ideal is to include five different cooking methods in one meal, so you might have griddled, poached, steamed, braised and fried food all at once. I'm not suggesting you specifically do this, of course, but that you think about the various components of a meal, bearing in mind a contrasting variety of colours and textures.

There are also considerations of setting and attitude. I read about these in *Washoku*, a fascinating cookbook by Elizabeth Andoh, an American who went to live in Japan. Two rather elevated phrases, coined by Sen no Rikyū, the 16th-century philosopher credited with refining the world of tea and the food served at the tea ceremony, sounded worth considering in all cooking. The first is *ichi go, ichi e* ('one moment, one meeting') which is about creating pleasure at one particular meal, a fleeting but special experience of shared cooking and eating. The other, which rings even truer to me, is *wabi-sabi* ('charm of the ordinary'), which is about the wonder of turning humble foodstuffs into simple but lovely meals (a thing that makes me happy on a daily basis).

All this is the antithesis of the worst western eating where, starving and mindless, you sink your teeth hungrily into a fast food burger. I'm not saying we should all become Zen about food or try to apply Japanese culinary principles, but once you start cooking with more vegetables, leaves and grains, there is a spirit in Japanese cooking that makes you produce better food, and makes you eat it in a more mindful way. Eating is not just about sating appetite but about appreciating, with all your senses, what is put before you, and honouring the ingredients with which it is made. I know this sounds a little bit Californian, but there is more to cooking and eating than ingredients and skill; there is an attitude that can make everything you serve, and everything you put in your mouth, taste better. And when you approach food this way, you eat less of it and you appreciate it more.

Now, if I could tap a little Japanese gong near your ear and give you a plateful of autumn chrysanthemums, I would.

33

# A IS FOR APPLE

An apple, the first fruit, is simple and comforting. 'A is for Apple' is one of the earliest things we learn. Looking at that cute, bright red fruit on the first page of our ABC, we associate it with safety, homeliness and domesticity. To me, its cheeky shape is endlessly cheering. As early as two years old, I would swing on the door of the greengrocer demanding 'wawos', my baby name for them. But the apple's symbolism is more complicated than a child can comprehend. In religion, mythology and fairy tales, there is both the good and the bad apple. From Adam and Eve to Snow White, the apple has seduced the innocent. Slice it horizontally and the five seedpods form a perfect pentagram, a shape sacred to both Christianity and sorcery and believed to hold the key to the knowledge of good and evil. Apples are also symbols of immortality and fertility. In England, a girl should put an apple under her pillow on

Hallowe'en night if she wants to dream of her husband-to-be; in Northern France the peel of an apple, twirled three times and thrown over the shoulder, is supposed to form the initial of a woman's future spouse. The apple stands for all fruits, is an emblem of fruitfulness itself.

American apple grower Frank Browning hits the nail on the head when he writes that apples 'are as common as toast, as elusive as dreams'. There are around eight thousand named varieties. But see them in the supermarket, reduced to a selection of pallid yellow (Golden Delicious) and bright green (Granny Smith), and you understand why most of us don't get excited about apples. We're largely unaware of their diverse flavours — aniseed, raspberryish and peachy — and buy them so far from their source that they hold little of the orchard's magic. But if you drive through apple-growing country, in Herefordshire, Normandy, New England or even the Norwegian fjords, it is impossible not to be moved by the apple's varied beauty. Crimson, tawny, ochre, russet, their colours hang heavily on the branch — a perfect metaphor for the bounty of the season — and their sweet odour scents a world otherwise smelling of smoke and decay.

The skin can be waxy and slippery, smooth or slightly sandy, but it should always be taut. The greatest pleasure is the first bite, when that skin gives way to juice — at once sweet and acidic — and a firm, glassy flesh that breaks with a crunch. You get to appreciate that there is an apple for every mood and as wide a range of flavours – the product of variety, weather, terroir and grower – as there is in wines. My own preference is for the tarter types. The jolt of acid-drop sourness you get from an Ashmead's Kernel is a wake-up call to the tastebuds. It's also worth looking out for the superb sweet-sour Adam's Pearmain, the Allington Pippin – which, though almost bitter in early autumn, will taste as honeyed as a quince by Christmas – and the aniseed-flavoured Ellison's Orange.

As well as eating apples raw, we cook them into cheering solace. Apples must appear in more homely puddings than any other fruit. Tarts, pies, crumbles, cakes, Austrian strudels, Eastern European *kolaches* and a profusion of American brown betties, pandowdies, buckles, grunts and slumps: you can never have too many apple pudding recipes. The apple's sweet acidity, often in conjunction with cider, can create some of the most comforting savoury dishes, too. Chicken or pheasant with apples and cream is deeply soothing, while the sight of apples baked around a joint of pork seems to stir something almost primordial in Sunday lunchers. I also like the Scandinavian and Russian habit of adding apple to herring in soured cream, or eating it with smoked fish and meat, as well as the Austrian use of *kren* – an apple and horseradish sauce – to go with *tafelspitz*, their version of pot-au-feu.

Compared to the apple, you have to feel sorry for the pear. Whenever I plunder the fruit bowl for a snack to give me a mid-afternoon boost, it will usually be the apple I fall for. The pear, whether long and elegant like the Conference, or deliciously dumpy like the Williams, looks shy and drowsy in comparison. After all, practically the whole of its body is in its bottom. I won't wake it now, I think. But the pear also has charm. While apples are brisk, pears are sensuous and other-worldly. They can be captured in glass cages in bottles of pear liqueur and have starring roles in nursery rhymes. I can fancy those golden bodies growing alongside silver nutmegs, or being delivered with a partridge on the first day of Christmas.

But actually, eating pears frustrates us, because they require patience. They are nearly always sold unripe because, fully mature, they are delicate creatures that not only bruise easily, but scar as they bump against sturdier beings. It's not commercially viable to sell them at their peak: you must watch and wait for that time and their period of optimum loveliness is fleeting. There's an old saying that one must be prepared to sit up at night to eat a ripe pear, its moment of perfection passes so quickly. Keep them at room temperature and don't be tempted to test for ripeness by prodding. Just press the fruit gently near the stem; if it gives a little, it is ready to eat. Test often, or maturity will come and go and you'll have missed the opportunity to bring out their full sweet pearness by eating them with some salty Roquefort or Gorgonzola, or on their own, the juices running down your arm. There is no pleasure in the grittiness of unripe pear flesh or the mealiness of over-ripe. But the good news is, it doesn't matter, because a carefully cooked pear is as good as the most perfect ripe one and there are endless things you can do with them: poaching them in white wine, red wine, cider, Marsala, cassis or ginger syrup; stuffing them with nuts; or baking them with cranberries. Pears are relatively cheap and, for cooking, ripe ones are too delicate, so those unyielding little bricks are perfect.

Once cooked, apples become fluffy or melting, depending on variety, while apricots and plums surrender completely. The glory of cooked pears is that the spoon still meets resistance as it slices the flesh, unctuous and satisfying, cutting through the network of softened membranes and fibres. And how that flesh absorbs the flavours around it! That much-derided dish of garnet beauties, pears in red wine, when cooked properly – slowly, then left to sit in the syrup to intensify both flavour and colour – is unrivalled in its capacity to be simple and luscious. If you're lazy, you don't even have to bother peeling pears. Go rustic and lay the halved fruits on their sides in a baking dish, pour over Marsala, add sugar, a couple of cinnamon sticks and some knobs of unsalted butter and bake slowly in the oven.

You'll have a wonderful mellow, warm, wintry dish to serve with vanilla ice cream.

The slender green-and-russet Conference pear is often recommended and it does have firm flesh and keeps its shape well, but I think it can be grainy and has a much less intense flavour the nearer you get to its core.

I like cooking with the pears that are also good to eat raw. Williams have the quintessential rounded pear shape, a lovely autumnal blush to the skin and taste distinctly musky. Doyenné du Comice, meaning 'top of the show', is the pear *par excellence*. Not even faintly gritty, it has perfumed, buttery flesh and is so juicy when ripe that you should eat it with a napkin standing by to mop up the stickiness. For a quiet, indulgent, unadulterated pear experience, this is the one to go for.

The dishes we cook with these fruits – pears in red wine, stewed apples with cream, pork chops with apple sauce – are gloriously old-fashioned, easy to make and rooted in the culinary culture of Northern Europe and North America. But the survival of all but the best-known varieties of apple and pear is seriously under threat, as commerce demands long shelf lives and blandness. The best way to honour these lovely fruits is to visit orchards and farmers' markets in search of old and lesser-known varieties. Though apples and pears are as common as toast, we yearn for flavours that are the stuff of dreams.

# 34

# SOUP IS NEVER DULL

Soup is just about the most sensible dish you can make. For a start it's based on stock that you can make with cooked, leftover bones. Food writers are forever exhorting us to use only what is spanking fresh, but I often make soup from carrots that are getting soft, or wilted salad. And leftover braises are a perfect base for a warming bowlful. But soup is not dull. A pot of soup is something you hug to yourself like a secret. Hurrying home on a cold day, you can feel miserable until you remember that there is soup in the house. The prospect is as cheering as being greeted by someone you love.

In our house, soup is often made on a Sunday night and eaten over the next few days. The carcass from the Sunday-lunch chicken is thrown into a pot with onion, carrot, celery, parsley and peppercorns, covered with water and simmered for a few hours. (Never add salt, skim the surface when it needs it and don't boil it, as that makes the stock murky.) The stock you use is paramount – your soup will only be as good as your stock – and judicious seasoning is also important, but a cookery course I did in my twenties opened my eyes to another important element.

We made a creamy vegetable soup (just leeks, potatoes and carrots), the prospect of which didn't particularly wow me, but it was one of the loveliest soups I have ever tasted. Why? The slow, careful sweating of the vegetables to bring out their sweetness. Of course, the butter you use adds greatly to the flavour but – in case your health alarm bells are ringing – you don't need much. Just melt enough to get the vegetables to exude their juices, cover the pan and regularly add splashes of water to keep everything moist and stop the vegetables from catching. In soups which are Mediterranean in tone, olive oil does the same job.

A bit of thought given to garnishes opens up new worlds, too. There is nothing wrong with a humble bowl of spiced lentil soup, but top it with yogurt and chilli-fried onions and you have a wonderful interplay of hot and cold. Flavoured creams – such as chilli for a pea and coriander soup, for example – can take your bowl to new heights, and embellishments, like chunks of ricotta or shavings of cheese, transform a plain dish into a special one. With careful sweating of the vegetables, good stock and judicious seasoning (with soup you have to taste, taste, taste, and a good squeeze of lemon juice will often heighten and bring the flavours together more than another scattering of salt), you can make a dish which hasn't broken the bank and somehow becomes more than the sum of its parts. Soup is a perfect example of sane and feel-good cooking.

# 35
# FRUITS OF LONGING

Figs, quince, pomegranates and dates: these are fruits that could turn a girl's head. Elusive, romantic and erotic, they conjure up visions of hot sun, starry skies and, let's be honest, sex. Figs are the sexiest of the lot.

Purple figs are the colour and texture of teenage love-bites, making you think of hungry kisses. One could even feel embarrassed handling figs in the wrong company. Soft and plump, it seems as though they are just waiting to be discovered, so delicate that you have to touch them gently and eat them before too many little beads of nectar form around the flower end. André Gide wrote that the fig had secrets, that it was a 'closed room where marriages are made,' while DH Lawrence got straight to the point. 'The Italians vulgarly say, it stands for the female part; the fig-fruit.' Well, yes. Figs are unquestionably sensual. They taste even better if they've been sitting in the sun; never eat them straight from the fridge. Warmth seems to bring out their delicate flavour and make their skin all the softer on your lips. Their main drawback is that a good fig is hard to find. Teasingly, they often promise more than they deliver. Their outside – be it black, purple, green or green-gold – gives no reliable clues. You may fall for a whole crate of beauties, only to find every specimen disappointingly dry. As in love, you have to hope. And keep trying...

When you do find perfect figs, leave them alone. Show off their lovely shape by serving a dozen on a platter at the end of a meal, or enhance their bloomy skin by setting them alongside a chalky goat's cheese. Cut each fruit in four and open it like a flower, fill with mascarpone and drizzle with lightly warmed honey, or serve with raspberries and a honey or lemon ice cream. Or fill a cooked tart shell with honeyed cream and arrange quartered fresh figs on top: a sugar plum fairy of a dessert.

Slightly under-ripe figs are for baking and will give you sweet and savoury dishes that are both elegant and earthy. Their little bodies really soak up juices and become fat with flavours: red wine with cinnamon, ginger, bay or thyme; white wine with a little cassis or rose water; orange juice with cardamom. Over-ripe figs – and they can get to that stage in the blink of an eye – are a good excuse to make a runny chutney, soft-set jam or the 'spoon sweets' of Greece and the Middle East: luscious fruits in syrup, eaten with little spoons and cups of thick black coffee.

The beauty of the fig disappears, at least superficially, when it's dried. It becomes gnarled and misshapen. But dried figs have their own allure. Deep and rich, they make a great autumnal stuffing. Pairing them with chocolate seems to restore some of their mystery: dried figs dipped in chocolate is a wickedly luxurious end to a wintry meal.

If the fig is young and untouched, the quince is all woman. Curvaceous but graceful, mature, comfortable with herself and resilient to knocks, a big honey-sweet mamma of a fruit. I can never believe how satisfyingly weighty, nor how gorgeously rounded, quince are in your hand. But the quince has a mystique, just as the fig does, partly because it's so ancient and partly because it's so hard to get hold of. You're lucky if you have a friend with a tree, or if you come across a big golden mound of them in a market or a Middle Eastern shop. They're never around for long enough to take for granted. And that scent – honey, musk and roses ('the smell of my sweetheart's breath', wrote the Andalusian-Arab poet, Shafer ben Utman al-Mushafi) – is hard to remember when the season ends.

All these fruits have to be handled properly to get the best out of them, but the quince needs the most work. Of course, you can fill a big bowl with them and enjoy their glow and fragrance for months, no cooking required, but you can't pick them up, toss them in the air and sink your teeth into them. Their hard acidic flesh has to be cooked, long and slow. Happily, they're so perfumed that you don't need to do anything complicated to them: poach them as you would pears, except for longer; parboil, slice and bake them covered in cream and sugar; add them to an apple sauce or a crumble. Raw, the flesh is as pale as an apple's; cooked slowly, it takes on a pinky hue that is beautiful beside a dollop of ice cream or Greek yogurt.

And the quince's honeyedness is astonishing (the Romans called the fruit *meli melum*, or 'honey apple'). Poached quince taste as though they've been steeped in Sauternes, so they're powerful enough to take on other distinctive flavours – cinnamon, cloves, star anise, saffron or even bay and rosemary – and they're well able to take their place in spicy fruit and meat stews, such as the tajines of Morocco or the *khoresht* of Persia.

Quince cheese, a thick, set preserve made by slowly cooking the whole fruit – skin, pips and all – then sieving and simmering the resulting purée with an equal quantity of sugar, is made all over the Mediterranean and eaten as a sweetmeat with coffee. It's the Spanish, who call it by the lyrical-sounding name membrillo, who really know how to enjoy this. They serve it in thin slices, like bits of rosy-hued glass, beside chunks of strong cheese. You can find membrillo in delis, but it's not cheap; better to bag your quince and spend a Saturday afternoon like some

Andalusian mistress, stirring your pot of amber jelly and filling the house with the smell of heaven.

To me, dates mean rafts of cushions and desert nights, probably because the boxes in which the fruits arrived in our house at Christmas when I was a child were decorated with *Boy's Own*-style sketches of camels and Bedouin tents. They brought a whiff of a world that Quality Street never could. Imagine how delighted I was to discover that deglat noor, the name of one of the finest varieties, means 'dates of light'. I used to think about eating these luscious fruits in the dark while listening to Maria Muldaur trilling through 'Midnight at the Oasis'. The earthbound reality was that I usually had rather dry dates, chopped up in brown bread sandwiches, for my school lunchbox. Well, they are very good with butter.

That tree of the sands, the date palm, drinks gallons of water from lakes below the ground, while the leaves provide sun canopies for trees of pomegranates, apricots and peaches. We think of dates as a luxurious extra, when for Bedouins they are fundamental. They can survive for days in the desert on dates and camel's milk. Small wonder that the fast of Ramadam is often broken with dates and a glass of water, or that dates are offered as a sign of friendship. There is a saying that the Bedouin spend their lives searching for 'the two black ones': water and dates. Dates are literally life-giving.

All over the Arab world, dates are made into exquisite sweetmeats and the fruits bring the same richness to savoury dishes as figs. Dates are great with pigeon, lamb and rice and are a revelation with oily fish. I've long since given up buying those Christmas boxes with their plastic spears, serving as harpoon and fake branch. Now I go for real branches of the fine, pale deglat noor, or the plump mahogany beads called medjool. Treat these dates simply. Serve them at the end of a meal with salty cheese or labneh, or with yogurt and honey, or with sliced oranges sprinkled with flower water and cinnamon. Or just offer mint tea and a tortoiseshell mix of dates on a plate: essence of the desert.

And then there's the pomegranate. 'Beautiful colour,' sighs my friend. 'Sin red.' Modern Greek books on dreams interpret pomegranates as a sign of temptation, sexual adventure, fertility and danger. They were, of course, the undoing of Persephone. Kidnapped by Pluto to be his bride in the underworld, she was allowed to return to Earth providing she hadn't eaten anything in Hades. But she hadn't been able to resist the pomegranate. She had eaten six seeds, so for six months Persephone had to stay as Queen of the Dead in Hades while the Earth mourned, only returning to Earth for the remainder of the year.

For the Greeks, the pomegranate is therefore double-edged: it embodies death and life. They eat the seeds in a kind of porridge of wheat and nuts at funerals, but also smash the fruits on their doorsteps at New Year in anticipation of spring.

Pomegranates don't mean spring to me; they are winter and Christmas. With their leathery skins and regal little calyxes, they look like something one of the Magi would have given. Or worn on his head. You don't even have to eat pomegranates to appreciate them. In December, they hang like great baubles from trees in Southern Italy, Turkey and Greece and arrive in markets with the Christmas lights.

Those seeds, glassy lozenges of tart sweet juice that burst against your tongue, are like jewels. Embedded in a beehive-like network of creamy pith, they can be deep garnet red or pale rose pink; nothing on the outside tells you which. Ask the vendor where the fruits are from: Spanish pomegranates have paler seeds and are sweeter; Middle Eastern fruits have redder seeds and a sourer flavour. Scattered on savoury salads of chicory and salty cheese, or sweet dishes of sliced oranges and ruby pink grapefruit, pomegranates bring magic. Mixed with sugar and rose water, or orange juice and orange blossom water, they make an impromptu dessert worthy of the *Arabian Nights*.

You can have something of pomegranate's tart, sour taste all year round with pomegranate molasses, an almost treacle-thick dark brown sauce made by boiling down the juice of the sourest specimens. A rich, acidic flavouring for braises, marinades and dressings, no Middle Eastern kitchen would be complete without it.

# 36
# OCTOBER IS MY FAVOURITE MONTH

October is my favourite month. I even like the shape of the word on the page. The 'O', because it's closed, suggests you'll be held, and indeed it's the 'settling down' month, the month when you turn back towards home. August allows – even demands – a lack of structure, odd meal times, even no meals at all (you might prefer just to down an icy draft of juice, then press the cold glass against your cheek). September is a month of beginnings: new shoes, empty exercise books, possibilities. In October, even before anyone has lit a bonfire, you smell smoke in the air and you want to taste it, too; I poach smoked haddock in milk and wonder if it's extravagant to buy a whole smoked duck. Gradually it gets colder. You pull a jumper on and realize that the world has shifted and you've returned to the kitchen. Of course I'm there in the summer, too, but only for brief stints, long enough to make a tomato salad or griddle chicken. Now, I take hold of it again and it feels like returning to someone you love. It might be because I was born in October – or maybe because I'm a bit of a hibernator – but I recognize the world at this time of year, I know its food, I like its smells and rhythms; October is where I'm from.

In Northern Ireland, where I grew up, October is the best month. Blackberries ripen later there, so we always went picking at the end of September and the beginning of October. We'd make a crumble before the fruit started to spoil; someone would be dispatched to the petrol station down the road (hub of gossip and emporium of everything you could possibly need) for vanilla ice cream and so the evening kicked off with pudding. By the end of the month, the trees' skeletons, stripped of their leaves, had appeared, and in the mornings they were white with frost. I loved the cold air filling my lungs as I walked past them on glittering tarmac on my way to school.

I start baking in October just because I want to be in the kitchen, sifting and weighing and doing things slowly. Bread dough rises, hands are covered in flour, your apron is never off. It isn't just dishes that change with the seasons, it's how you cook, how you want to move round the kitchen. Come autumn, I cook as if on autopilot, as if my body remembers what to do. When I brown meat for a braise – turning it over and adjusting the heat so that it gets just the right amount of caramelization – I barely think about it. Later in the process, I know when – and by how much – to move the lid on the casserole, nudging it so that the stock around the meat can reduce.

This is different from spring and summer cooking, when you have to be nimble, turning fillets of salmon just at the moment the skin is golden and crispy but not scorched. Autumn cooking is not about instant flavours or assemblies of startling contrasts, it's about layering and waiting.

Then, of course, there's October's food: sweet pumpkins, milky hazelnuts, drowsy-looking pears, plump mussels in their inky shells. You can re-embrace dried foods too. I no longer stand holding a bag of lentils thinking it's too warm to cook them; instead they're turned into Middle Eastern purées or Indian dals, or tossed in mustardy dressings.

October also brings Hallowe'en. Some decry it as an American import, but it's actually an Irish festival (19th-century Irish immigrants took it to the States). The best party I ever gave was as an eleven-year-old one Hallowe'en. We weren't allowed fireworks in Northern Ireland because of the Troubles, and there you carve lanterns from turnips (no easy task) not pumpkins; the turnip smelled bitter as its flesh became singed inside. My dad lit a bonfire and we put out platters of fat sausage rolls and sticky pork ribs on the dining room table. Kenny, our family butcher, came with his guitar and sang Johnny Cash and Burl Ives songs (he thought 'Big Rock Candy Mountain' was good, because it was a tease, but we all preferred 'Ring of Fire'). We sat on the floor eating apple and blackberry crumble. This is such a good party, I thought, a party of bonfires and smoke and fruit and lanterns and warmth.

It could only have happened in October.

# FROM RUSSIA WITH LOVE

Imagine a table laid with a linen cloth, covered with bowls and small plates of all the delicacies that Russia and Eastern Europe has to offer: cured herrings, smoked fish, pickled cucumbers and peppers, fiery crimson radishes, winter-cold soured cream, cheeses, brined mushrooms, caviar, rare beef with horseradish, beetroot purée, preserved plums and rye bread. This is the *zakuski* table – the table of 'little bites' – the Russian version of Middle Eastern mezze, Spanish tapas and Italian antipasti. Indeed, it is such a feast that it often becomes the whole meal.

Most credit Peter the Great for bringing this style of eating to Russia. He had certainly seen enough Scandinavian smörgåsbords (which the *zakuski* table resembles), while travelling and waging war, to have adopted the idea. This table of plenty says much about Russian hospitality. It is well known that, even in times of want (and they've had plenty of those), Russian hosts pull out all the stops to produce a feast. A spread of *zakuski* can include the most luxurious items (in Gogol's *Dead Souls*, the chief of police offers delights which include an amazing pie made with the head and cheeks of 300lb of sturgeon), or it can be limited to the most frugal: a few herrings, some radishes, black bread and pickles.

*Zakuski* became particularly popular in the 19th century and were served according to strict guidelines. Elena Molokhovets's *Classic Russian Cooking* (the Russian bible of cooking and household management, published in 1861) contains illustrations showing how to arrange the various elements. The key thing was to serve *zakuski* on an oval or round table, either beside the main dining table or in an anteroom. The table had to be placed away from the wall, so that guests could walk round it. Carafes of vodka were in the centre, surrounded by bread and mounds of unsalted butter, and the various *zakuski* were placed around the edges.

There is an abundance of dishes that are just right for this kind of meal. Apart from Russian and Eastern European foods, there are also some Middle Eastern dishes which are perfect: pickled aubergines, aubergine purée, a purée of roast pepper with pomegranate molasses and walnuts, plus Italian cured beef and – a regular on *zakuski* tables as Russians adore Georgian food –

kidney beans in Georgian plum sauce. These all work with no dissonant notes, even though they come from different cultures.

To make a spread of *zakuski*, you need an array of homemade dishes, then add bought produce and simple foods – cured ham, spicy dried sausage, hard-boiled eggs, warm waxy potatoes and salmon roe – and you have a feast right for both the depths of winter and the brightness of spring. Choose your dishes according to the season, and, in the colder months, add some hot dishes too, such as warm roast pork belly and savoury pies.

You don't have to lay out your *zakuski* according to tradition, just make your table as rich and varied as possible, choose your most beautiful cloth and glassware and pack your freezer with vodka. Food is sometimes about fantasy and romance, and there's nothing wrong with being Anna Karenina for an evening…

# 38

# I CAN NEVER RESIST PUMPKINS

Pumpkins and squash seem the perfect symbol of autumn and winter cooking. The cook has the job of getting through that tough skin before finding the tender flesh, and they give of their best only after slow cooking. But it's worth it. They are great culinary chameleons, able to soak up and marry well with ingredients as diverse as Gruyère, chipotles, rosemary, sage and nutmeg. Their smoky, sweet flavours are just right for the season of turning leaves.

Confusion reigns, however, about the difference between a pumpkin and a squash. It is a difficult area and often local usage dictates what is a squash and what is a pumpkin. Both are members of the same family and, although the terms are often used interchangeably, pumpkins are usually the jack-o'-lantern shape we associate with Hallowe'en, with thick orange skin, while squashes can be smooth, warty, striped, stippled, their skins as green and shiny as old leather books, pale yellow, flame orange, or delicate amber. They come in myriad shapes – acorns, turbans, melons and curled, snake-like creatures – and sizes.

Each year, I display them before I cook them: a row is lined up on the kitchen table; a great big *Rouge Vif d'Etampes*, the French variety that looks like Cinderella's carriage and acts as a doorstop between kitchen and living room; little miniature ones with cute names such as Munchkin, Jack-be-Little and Baby Boo sit among the candles on the mantelpiece. Their flesh, once cooked, can be as smooth as that of avocados or baked quince, the flavour as sweet as corn, or, admittedly, simply bland, if you end up with a bad specimen.

The important matter for the cook is to find a variety you like, be it a pumpkin or a squash. The best all-rounder, to my mind, is Crown Prince. It's an elegant grey blue, the sort of colour you might find on a chart of historic paints, with not a hint of the vivid golden flesh inside. The ubiquitous butternut squash always has a sweet flavour and melting flesh, while the chubby, yellow-and-green striped Sweet Dumpling and Delicata are both excellent for stuffing and baking. Cut the top off these little ones and, once you've scooped out the seeds and fibres, fill them with mushrooms, cream and cheese, a part-cooked stuffing of wild and brown rice, dried cranberries and smoked bacon, or chopped cooked spinach and ricotta. Replace the lids and roast them wrapped in foil to stop the sweet juices from running out in the roasting tin and burning.

Even if I'm going to purée the flesh, I either roast wedges or sauté chunks in butter rather than boiling them. You need to drive off about one-third of their moisture to intensify their taste and, anyway, pumpkin flesh loves butter, olive oil and cream; you will seldom eat a low-calorie pumpkin dish.

The Italians cook pumpkin and squash in risotto, or mash the flesh, sweeten it with crushed amaretti and use it to stuff pasta. The Belgians cook a *carbonade* of beef and beer in a hollowed-out pumpkin; in South-West France they roast wedges with goose fat and thyme. In America, there's an endless list of pumpkin and squash pies and tarts, both sweet and savoury. I love savoury pumpkin tarts filled with salty cheeses – Gorgonzola, Gruyère or feta. The oldest pumpkin seeds were found in Mexico, and they make one of the most ancient pumpkin recipes, *calabaza en tacha*, candied pumpkin, which is part of the Día de los Muertos celebrations. Cooked in brown sugar, orange juice and cinnamon (it's delicious with star anise too), it's sometimes eaten for breakfast.

Then there is pumpkin soup. Using a base recipe of chopped pumpkin or squash sweated in butter with chopped leeks and simmered in stock, I turn out endless variations every autumn. Make it with a good splash of bourbon, scattering the top with smoked bacon, serve it under a melting cheese crust or season it with pickle juice, paprika and dill (a gorgeous Austrian idea).

Pumpkins, because I didn't see any until I was about twenty-three, are still a novelty to me. I see the image of the girls in Laura Ingalls Wilder's *Little House* books using them as stools to sit on in the attic. American friends, who find pumpkin and squash so mundane, exclaim, 'Oh, you and your pumpkins,' but I will always love them. With pumpkins, the only limit is the cook's imagination.

# 39

# THE FAT OF THE LAND

Pork is the meat I most associate with winter. Its succulent fattiness keeps out the cold and the dishes we cook with it are satisfying and gutsy rather than refined. Its closest companions – apples, dried fruit, beans and lentils, mustard, juniper, cabbage, caraway and maple syrup – are also good autumn and winter ingredients. If you have these to hand and a good source of well-bred pork, you have a feast.

We love pork's sweet fattiness, its almost gamey taste and the joy of salty crackling. The European and American canon of classic dishes is one long line of porkers: rough country pâtés and pork fillet with prunes in France; poached Italian sausage with beans and *mostarda*; loin of pork studded with caraway and served with sauerkraut in Austria; sweet-glazed spare ribs in the US; roast pork with apple sauce in Britain and Ireland.

And across Europe there are more hams, sausages and salamis than you ever thought possible.

Pigs are like humans: gregarious yet independent, with a desire to be surrounded by companions and hungry for any food that is put in front of them. Their IQ is on a par with that of dogs. They can be taught to perform tasks such as truffle hunting and can recognize their owners. Few animals arouse such feelings in farmers and much has been written about the difficulty of slaughtering family pigs that are regarded as pets. Tomi Ungerer, in his book *Far Out Isn't Far Enough* – an account of his time spent on a small homestead in rural Nova Scotia – writes that pig-killing was a popular topic of conversation among neighbours, but that it was considered bad luck, even rude, to use the word 'pig'. The pig was more commonly referred to as 'Mr Dennis', so someone might comment: 'My mother, when we killed Mr Dennis, she locked herself in the house and played the harmonium.' We get emotional about pigs, perhaps because they remind us of ourselves.

Pigs are now raised and slaughtered all year round, but in the past (and even now in some parts of Europe), the autumnal pig-killing day was a cause for celebration. The day of slaughter is mystical. The more carefully nurtured the pig, the greater the joy at eating and using every part, and the hams and salumi that result feed country families all through the winter.

But most of the pork we eat comes from pigs raised using intensive methods. In much modern pig farming, these sociable creatures are not allowed to roam or forage for food outside, as is their natural wont, but are confined to such small areas that the company of others is a torment. They get depressed, which shows itself in bar-biting. Injuries, particularly to the ears and tail, are common as the pigs get stressed. As well as being cruel, this kind of farming produces meat that is flabby and tasteless. Instead of the varied diet they naturally prefer, factory-farmed pigs are fed on the same food pellets every day, are reared to grow fast and, because of the risk of infection due to the close confines in which they live, can be filled with antibiotics. Modern breeds have also been bred to have less fat, thus removing one of the main providers of succulence and flavour. But we don't have to eat pork like this.

With more small farmers looking for quality and flavour, it is possible to find pork that has been reared humanely, allowed to graze and given a varied diet by a caring farmer. If it is from one of the 'rare breed' pigs – such as Berkshire, Gloucester Old Spot, Saddleback, Tamworth or Middle White – then you're doing even better. When you find a butcher who can tell you how the pork he sells has been reared and what breed it is, treasure him and be happy to pay the price asked for this superior meat.

Otherwise, find a farm where you can source your pork directly, and don't let your buying standards drop when you're looking for bacon, ham or sausages.

We tend to be a bit unadventurous when it comes to cooking pork, sticking to the ubiquitous chop, perhaps because we are confused about which cuts should be used for what. As far as fresh pork goes, the best joints for roasting are the loin and leg. The shoulder, a cheaper cut, is great for slow-roasting, while the belly, with its lovely layering of fat, produces an exquisitely sweet mouthful and great crackling. It can also be boned and stuffed, and is the cut that provides spare ribs and the meat for pork terrines and pâtés. Salted, it is what the French serve in slices with lentils and mustard sauce to make the bistro classic, *petit salé*.

Pork fillet is completely lean and needs to be cooked quickly, either roasted (though it needs copious basting), or sautéed in medallions or escalopes. One of my mum's best dishes is pork escalopes battered with a mallet, coated with egg and breadcrumbs and fried: delicious with sautéed potatoes and a good dollop of English mustard. Chops can be cut from the loin, but are even tastier if they're from the shoulder, as they have good marbling (these are known as spare rib chops). The knuckle or hock is cheap and largely overlooked. Fresh, salted or smoked, it's wonderfully gelatinous and hits the bliss spot when cooked slowly and served with lentils or beans.

Hams are made from the hind leg and are cured by salting and drying, sometimes smoking as well. They come in two forms: one that is 'raw' but ready-to-eat, such as Parma ham, and another that requires further cooking, such as the ham which – glazed with sugar and mustard and studded with cloves – traditionally adorns the Christmas table. Bacon, which comes from the back or the belly of the pig, is also cured and can be smoked.

Coming downstairs to the smell of frying bacon is one of the best starts to the day. When staying at my grandparents' farm when I was a child, the morning always began with my granny making potato bread or soda farls at the kitchen table and thick rashers of bacon spitting on the stove. If we are demanding about the pork we eat, a good breakfast fry-up like this will remain a reality, not a nostalgic food memory.

# 40
# THE COMFORT OF BEANS

Nothing provides quite as much culinary succour as beans. I will never forget the first time I made cassoulet, the classic dish of South-West France. Rhythmically layering the par-boiled beans with big handfuls of parsley and thyme, chunky Toulouse sausages, sweet breast of lamb and salty duck confit was soothing. Periodically stirring the pot to distribute the breadcrumb crust that forms on the top and acts as a thickener for the dish, I saw those firm white beans turn into the softest pot of food.

It's a pity we don't cook beans more often. Perhaps the soaking time puts us off: around eight hours, though 'overnight' seems to be the rule of thumb. You need to think ahead to have your soaked beans ready for a dish, though the quick-soak method means you can enjoy beans on the same day as you get the urge to eat them. (Bring your beans to the boil, take them off the heat and leave them to soak for two hours.) Beans take time to cook, too, but you are rewarded with a melting mass that absorbs any flavour with which they are cooked: pork and lamb, olive oil, duck fat, garlic, tomatoes, onions or herbs. In France, as well as the South-West's cassoulet-style dishes based on beans cooked with pork or duck, the Bretons and Normans pair haricot and flageolet beans with lamb.

You would think Eastern Europeans lived on bean soups, looking at how many there are in their repertoire. Beans also appear in side dishes there, especially with cabbage, and there's the Hungarian-style cassoulet, *sólet*. Tuscans are supposed to be the bean-eaters of Italy, but you find plenty of beans in the North-East as well, particularly in the smoked bacon and cabbage soup, *jota*. In New England, debate rages from Boston to small-town Maine about how to cook baked beans and what variety of beans to use, while local historical societies hold bean-in-the-hole bakes where beans are cooked in underground pits for twenty-four hours, just as they were in the past.

Haricot beans, which are also known as navy beans, are probably the most popular of all dried beans. They are small and white, not too starchy and are used for baked beans and cassoulet (if you're in France, try to find the slightly larger *Soissons*). Cannellini beans are very similar to haricot, but a little bit bigger, with a fluffier texture, while the flageolet is pale green with a creamy texture and delicate flavour.

Borlotti beans, which are also known as cranberry beans, are large and pink-speckled and, to me, have a slight flavour of gammon. Butter beans, my least favourite, are big starchy beans with a thick skin and a potato-y flavour. They disintegrate easily, so do be careful when cooking them, but they're good with strong flavours such as mustard and chorizo. Red kidney beans are mealy, with a distinctive meaty flavour, and are used a lot in Georgian cooking to make salads for their *zakuski* (little mezze-style dishes): beans cooked with coriander and fenugreek is one of the best-known Georgian dishes.

There are a few key things to look out for when dealing with dried beans. Try to make sure they're not more than six months old; older than that and they take longer to cook and some very ancient ones will never soften. Cook them in just enough water to cover, but don't drown them, and cook them slowly. The best method is in a covered pan in a low oven – they seem to break up less and become more creamy – but slowly on the stove top is okay. Keep checking them towards the end of cooking, as age, length of soaking time and variety all affect how long they need to cook. A bit of salt pork, pork fat or olive oil, onion slices, spices and herbs all give vital flavouring.

On the subject of seasoning, whether to salt beans or not – it was long thought that salt would toughen beans if you added it during cooking – is still a matter of debate. J Kenji López-Alt, an American food writer with a scientific slant, has conducted experiments on cooking beans: both adding salt and leaving the beans unsalted. He found that the skins of unsalted beans are more likely to burst during cooking, while the skins of salted beans stay more intact (though they are not tough). There are times when you want beans to collapse more, and times when you don't. I want them to stay intact if I'm cooking them to use in salads, for instance. The choice is yours...

Some lentils need soaking, but others don't, so check how you should treat each variety. Split red lentils can soften in as little as fifteen minutes and they make a superb soup when added to ham stock, just stir some shreds of ham into it before serving.

There are also large green or brown lentils, which are whole and unskinned and therefore retain their shape, though I usually hang the expense and go for Puy or Umbrian lentils, the small green-grey ones, the *grands crus* of the lentil world. They're fantastic with sausages and Italian *mostarda* or sweet-and-sour figs, or with pot-roast guinea fowl, monkfish or smoked haddock. I usually cook them with sautéed onion, carrot, celery and pancetta in light chicken stock, though they also take well to being cooked in wine, or having mustard and cream added at the end. Cooked quite plainly and then doused in vinaigrette (dress them while still warm so they absorb the flavours), they make wonderful salads.

Lentils and beans have become increasingly hip, especially the posher ones. The reaction you get from family and friends as you lift the lid off a dish of cassoulet or a pot of maple-baked beans on a cold winter's day shows how much we yearn for them.

# 41

# WILD THINGS

It took me a while to get used to game. Though country born and bred, I am not from a hunting and shooting family. Game would enter our house as gifts. When my dad arrived home with a handful of pheasants – I was about five years old at the time – their bodies still warm, their eyes beady and open, their feathers beautiful but blotched with markings as dark and mysterious as those of a jungle animal, I screamed the house down. This was real food and it was frightening.

Game is very different to farmed meat. It tastes of the earth, the result of a diet of berries, wild grain, grass and grubs; no wonder we describe it as 'strong'. Then there's its dense meat and sinewy body, the result of a life of hard work and freedom. The cook needs to work respectfully – basting, barding, moistening – to bring the animal to tenderness. Put game in a pot with the time-honoured flavourings of wine, onions and herbs and you end up with rich, assertive, muscular food.

If you've shot the game yourself, you have the added pleasure – similar to dealing with home-grown vegetables – of procuring your own food: a basic, age-old pride that is almost instinctive and links us to the past.

Time spent in France brought me round to game. On school exchanges there in my teens, the men of the house would go off quietly with their guns and be proud of the rabbits they brought back. These tasted so good – golden-fleshed after being pot-roasted in an old casserole with bacon, rosemary and a splash of wine – that it was impossible not to hope the hunts would be successful.

Hunting for, and cooking, game seems natural to me, as long as the hunt is not a booze-fuelled bash in which killing is more important than getting food.

Not all game is truly wild nowadays. In order to maintain stock for organized shoots, pheasants and partridges are bred before being released. Properly wild birds are all types of wild duck, grouse, pigeon, woodcock and snipe. The quail, still widely regarded as game, is not found wild in Britain at all, though it is still shot in parts of Eastern Europe. Here it's farmed and real game aficionados scorn it, but I'm fond of the little birds. The flavour may be mild, but quails still make for good eating: there are plenty of small bones to get your chops around, they cook quickly and look elegant. Rabbit is also rather looked down on, but it tastes better than chicken and works with many different flavours. Farmed venison is just as good as the wild stuff, as both kinds graze, the farmed animals are not forced to grow at unreasonable rates, and all venison farms hang their meat. In times when much meat tastes bland, autumn and winter servings of venison, pheasant and rabbit shouldn't just be for special occasions, but a regular part of our diet.

When cooking game, the key issue is to stop it becoming dry. Don't marinate it in red wine before cooking, as many recipes instruct. The alcohol draws out moisture; you might as well pickle the meat. Marinating it in herbs or spices moistened with olive oil is much better. As a rule, cook it quickly at a high heat, or slowly at a very gentle pace, larding it with fat, or cooking it with bacon, and basting often.

There is a machismo to game-eating. Many are the stories about pheasant so high it parted company from its head as it was hanging, and I've eaten with men so intent on gamey grouse that I could hardly bear to be at the same table. Girly though it may be, I prefer my game subtly flavoured. One of the good things about game is that it is not a standardized product. If you buy it from a good butcher or dealer, you have a say in how strong a flavour you want, depending on how long it has been hung.

The hunt for mushrooms is of an entirely different order. It is the silent hunt and the hiddenness of the hunting ground is one of the great attractions of mushroom picking. Scandinavians talk about 'secret places' and the French refer to their hunting grounds as *nids*, or 'nests'. Fungi are mysterious and magical, inhabiting a world of leaves and mulch. They have distinctive personalities: vibrantly coloured umbrellas, toadstool-shaped houses, little brown pigs or porcini, chanterelles – looking like yellow-skirted ballerinas – and little bearded men.

My best mushrooming trips have been in France, leaving with friends first thing in the morning (the best time to pick) with flasks of warm food and wine. We're not too serious, we just want enough mushrooms to fry up that evening and we take as much pleasure in the environment – the bosky smell in our nostrils and the sun beginning to filter through the trees – as we do in the mushrooms. And yet the hunt gets under your skin. You become completely focused on the mushrooms in a way that is almost meditative.

Ceps, known in Italy as porcini and in Britain as penny buns, are the kings of the mushroom world. With a dark brown cap and a swollen stem, they have the most pronounced meaty flavour. If you're lucky enough to get big ceps, grill them whole, or bake them, stuffed with breadcrumbs, garlic and parsley. Chanterelles are more delicate creatures, egg-yolk yellow, trumpet-shaped and with a slight smell of apricots. Both these types of fungi dry well and there is nothing wrong with replacing wild mushrooms in a recipe with a mixture of dried wild and fresh cultivated ones.

Fresh wild mushrooms are now more available commercially, but, since they're not cheap, you'll want to treat them properly. Don't buy any that are slimy, withered or broken. Clean them with a soft brush and cook them as soon as possible, though a day in the fridge in a paper bag isn't the end of the world.

Even a simple sauté has to be done with care. Cook the mushrooms first in a little hot oil, then reduce the heat and add butter for flavour. Mushrooms can throw off a lot of moisture, which is fine if you are making a sauce, but if you want them to be drier then continue to cook them until the moisture has evaporated. Add a little cream and sherry or Madeira for a sauce to eat with guinea fowl or pasta, make them into one of the most luxurious omelettes, or add a little garlic and parsley and serve straight from the pan.

# 42

# MONSIEUR MATUCHET PLAYS THE PIANO

Backpacking was never my thing. In my early twenties, when friends were setting off for long stints exploring Asia, I was planning intricate journeys around regional France. The *Good Hotel Guide* – most of whose hotels I couldn't afford – was my bedtime reading, along with Patricia Wells's *The Food Lover's Guide to France*. I studied the descriptions of my favourite hotels so often that, these days, I'm not sure which I stayed in and which I didn't. (If you read about a place often enough, I find, you might as well have visited.)

The Lot Valley and the Dordogne – an area which seemed to have more *plus beaux villages de France* than any other – became my dream destination. I wanted cassoulet and walnuts, duck confit and prunes.

Driving down through France with my then-boyfriend, finally on our way there, the people we met confirmed that we were heading for the right place. '*On mange bien là-bas*,' they said. The colours changed as we travelled, until we were surrounded by shades of honey, ochre, terracotta and the green-gold of burrs.

Our first night was spent in St-Cirq-Lapopie, a medieval *village-perché*, in a hotel just under André Breton's house. The bedroom was tiny; it had uneven whitewashed walls and a small window that looked out on to the Lot below. The ceiling, a chalky azure painted with little gold stars, was so enchanting it nearly took precedence over dinner. I'll just stay here, I thought, and lie on the white bedcover looking at the stars and thinking about walnuts.

Monsier Matuchet – the hotel's owner and an Alain Delon lookalike – showed us into the dining room. On a rough-hewn table there were sweet-smelling Charentais melons, a huge ham, bottles of walnut oil and Armagnac, jars of duck confit and a big earthenware bowl of booze-soaked prunes. All the food came from nearby and made you realize that the countryside here wasn't just beautiful, it was hardworking. I stopped thinking of the place as postcard bucolic and started to see what anchored it.

The menu – which Monsieur Matuchet talked us through – was one of those perfect short affairs you get in France that have only two choices at every course. Even though it was early September, and summer was still hanging around, the kitchen was in full autumnal swing: there were salads of smoked duck and wild mushrooms with duck gizzards, a pork and bean stew, duck breast with the potent walnut and garlic sauce *aillade*, figs with hazelnut ice cream.

Monsieur Matuchet, creator of star-speckled ceilings, was also in charge of the kitchen. It was honest, unflashy cooking, yet the cuisine of South-West France is so burdened by the image of foie gras and cassoulet – the first deemed too luxurious, the other too gutsy for modern stomachs as well as too time-consuming to make – that it's not raved about by home cooks here in the way that, say, Provençal cooking is. It's seen as heavy and old-fashioned. But when autumn comes round, I think about Monsieur Matuchet and the rich-but-homely food he produced that night.

The American food writer, Paula Wolfert, has written about 'front-of-the-mouth food' – complex, innovative dishes that dazzle but whose charms quickly evaporate – and also its opposite, 'evolved' food, cooking based on ingredients that have a natural affinity with each other, dishes that honour the spirit of a particular region. Evolved cooking is what you find in South-West France, and it encompasses far more than foie gras and cassoulet. Duck legs with prunes, garlic-studded pork, Armagnac-scented apple tarts... these make for better eating on the cool, gauzy days of autumn than any plate of roasted Mediterranean vegetables. They are dishes with length and depth of flavour.

I wasn't surprised that most of the people in the dining room that night were French. The only other tourists, an American couple with wide-brimmed hats that they wore to dinner, kept smiling at us as if to acknowledge our shared luck in finding this gem of a place.

Monsier Matuchet's menu was do-able. I know this because, as soon as the main courses were served, Monsieur M was able to leave the kitchen and show off another of his talents. He took to the piano and played jazz (of course he did). It made me love the place all the more. The Americans smiled.

# 43
# GATHERING IN

Most nuts are grown in warm areas, but, as with spices and dried fruits, countries with colder climates have adopted them as emblems of the bounty of autumn and the stores of winter. In Central European coffee houses from Prague to Vienna, hazelnuts, chestnuts and walnuts stud gâteaux and fill pastries, while nuts appear at Christmas in every Northern European country, as dependable as the fat man in the red coat.

Hazelnuts are the sweetest of nuts. They are the sopranos – small, smooth, high-pitched – to the walnut's deep bass notes. A cake made with walnuts seems earthed, a quality that makes you feel safe and content; the same cake made with hazelnuts feels more jaunty. Hazelnuts start off milky and juicy in early autumn and become sweet and almost toasty after months of ripeness. They're good in many recipes in which you might otherwise use walnuts: salads of smoked duck, with blue and Gruyère-type cheeses, with apples and pears, in cakes, biscuits and ice creams. The Italians love them, but the French Savoie is the area where I've found them most used. Here, pasta parcels are stuffed with hazelnuts and pumpkin, while trout are stuffed with hazelnuts and mushrooms. Hazelnuts are also stirred into ice creams and incorporated into shortbread and tarts.

Walnuts are the royalty of the nut world. This noble nut doesn't have the pale, aristocratic elegance of the almond, but it is king, both in terms of its widespread use and in its deep, meaty flavour, which comes mainly from the tannins in the skin. If you can, catch some at the early 'wet' stage, when they are creamy, with a golden papery skin covering the two perfect halves of their coruscated kernel. The walnut tree is held in particularly high esteem in the Dordogne. For peasant families, they were a dependable crop – an assurance of prosperity – and they are still one of the most important products of the region. In the past, autumn evenings were spent on *l'énoisement*, or nut shelling, when family members told stories and sang songs. It is said that every bit of the walnut was used except the noise it makes as it is cracked. Walnuts that were not kept for eating were mixed with water, heated and pressed for their oil, as they still are. The cookery of the area is suffused with the flavour of walnuts: the oil is used to dress salads, though always in conjunction with a milder oil as walnut oil is strong; the nuts are scattered over leaves, pressed into sourdough bread slathered with Roquefort, or tossed with green beans. A digestif is made by infusing red wine, sugar and marc with tender young walnut leaves, and a liqueur from macerating fresh walnuts in eau de vie, delicious as a flavouring for ice cream or drizzled over poached pears.

Georgians adore walnuts too, using them in dishes that have been adopted by Russian cooks. Georgians stuff fish with walnuts and pomegranate seeds and make sauces by pounding walnuts with pomegranate molasses and roasted red peppers, or coriander and beetroot. If you are looking for unusual uses for the nut, Italy also boasts a few lesser-known sauces. *Salsa delle api*, made with ground walnuts, honey and mustard moistened with stock, is served with boiled meats in Piedmont, while Ligurians make *salsa di noci*, a kind of walnut pesto.

The pecan, the nut of a variety of hickory tree, is as American as apple pie. American cookbooks are full of uses for them, particularly in stuffings, salads, tarts and old-fashioned puddings such as buckles, cobblers and slumps. Pecans may look like walnuts, apart from their skin, which is the colour of red squirrels, but their flavour is much sweeter, reminiscent of the burnt sugariness of maple syrup. Pecans, like maple syrup, seem to marry well with coffee; each flavour enhances the other, so a plate of pecan cookies or a wedge of pecan cake always goes down well with an afternoon brew.

Chestnuts, their polished mahogany bodies bursting through their green prickly coats, are so beautiful that you long to like them. But you have to venture further than partnering them with Brussels sprouts for that to happen. My chestnut devotion developed when I started to cook chestnuts with meat. Try sticking them into a pan of sausages braised with shallots and prunes, or putting them alongside a roast joint of pork, and you'll see why I was converted. Now I love their haunting sweetness and fudgy texture. Vacuum-packed cooked chestnuts are a great standby, but nothing beats the woody taste of freshly roasted nuts. Pierce the skin and roast the nuts in the oven, with a few tablespoons of water, for ten minutes. Remove the outer skins, then simmer the nuts in a mixture of water and oil until the inner skins start to come off. Scoop them up, wrap in a cloth and, while still warm, rub to remove the skins.

Although they are now regarded as a special ingredient we buy at Christmas, chestnuts used to be the food of the poor, a staple for peasants in the non-grain-producing areas of South-West France and parts of Italy. Wild chestnuts were used to make flour and the chestnut tree was often referred to in France as *l'arbre à pain*, or the 'bread tree'. In many regions, chestnuts are still regarded as everyday fare. In Northern Italy, you'll find them in countless risottos, stewed with venison and juniper, braised with lentils and – the greatest revelation – in salads with cured pork and spicy sausage. The French use chestnuts for soups, stuffings and vegetable dishes such as chestnut gratin. They can't get enough of them in Central Europe either. The Hungarians are particularly chestnut crazy. Roasting chestnuts at home is not unusual there and chestnut purée seems to be as ubiquitous as paprika.

Nuts are ancient and the activity of eating them propels us back to age-old behaviour. Most of us don't go foraging in the woods for them, but we at least rifle through bags of hazelnuts and walnuts each Christmas, cracking them one by one. They bring a sense of the outside into the home.

# WINTER ON MY TONGUE

It was snowing so hard on our journey from Copenhagen airport that news reports threatened road closures. Skaters were wheeling round the outdoor ice rink in the central square and a little kiosk was doing a roaring trade selling *glögg*, the Scandinavian mulled wine rich with almonds and raisins. Given the weather and the late hour, we decided to see what room service in the hotel could rustle up. Half an hour later, they brought a tray laden with hot slices of pork belly on caraway-scented rye bread, spiced pickled prunes, cucumber, warm potatoes in soured cream and dill and glasses of cold, golden beer: flavours of winter in a northern climate.

Many spices and herbs used in the north come from hot-weather countries. Even dill, the most prominent flavouring in Scandinavian food, is native to the Mediterranean and is used with abandon in Turkey and Iran.

Walking along the streets of Stockholm or Copenhagen, your nose is alert to the scent of cardamom, cinnamon and caraway coming from the pastries and breads in the cafés and *konditorier*. In Austria, aniseedy caraway speckles pork casseroles and roasted root vegetables, while in Scandinavia it flavours schnapps and rye bread. Horseradish, which we British only get out to partner roast beef, is mixed with cranberries, bread and beetroots to make Russian sauces for boiled beef and roast pork. On the Swedish smörgåsbord table, that tongue-tingling mixture of hot and cold dishes, allspice, mustard and horseradish are used in marinades for herrings, and all over Scandinavia you find salmon cured under a snowdrift of salt and sugar and fronds of head-clearing dill.

Look at caraway, ginger and cardamom on a balmy day and you'll be transported to India or Morocco; but on days when you can see your breath form clouds in the freezing air, they take us to Scandinavia, Russia, Austria, Hungary and even Northern Italy instead.

Friuli-Venezia Giulia in North-East Italy is one of the most fascinating regions for seeing how warm-country flavourings have been harnessed in a cold climate. The food is unlike that from any other region of Italy. The country has been home to three great spice ports: Genoa, Venice and Trieste. The Genoese never welcomed foreign spices into their kitchens and just a few appear in Venetian dishes, but Friuli-Venezia Giulia embraced exotic flavours, many of them coming from Trieste, a port of entry and exit for the spices and coffee used in the Austro-Hungarian empire. It's hardly surprising that a few of them were incorporated into the area's cooking.

Snowed in one Christmas in Friuli, it was hard to be sure exactly where I was, as I enjoyed goulash of beef cheeks spiced with Hungarian paprika, cabbage flavoured with caraway and hams cured with juniper. Here, little bread dumplings are accompanied by a sauce of cucumber, soured cream, paprika and dill, cloves flavour onions and pasta is served with ricotta dusted with cinnamon. Horseradish is a signature flavouring of this part of North-East Italy, too. Look for a sandwich in this area and you're more likely to find a poppy seed roll filled with ham or pork and freshly grated horseradish than a tomato-and-mozzarella-stuffed panino.

Friuli is the only part of Italy where poppy seeds, so prevalent in the baking of Central and Eastern Europe, are widely used. You can enjoy them here in chocolate cakes rich with cinnamon and cloves, sprinkled over pasta and gnocchi, or used as a filling for strudel. Central Europeans make cakes so dense with poppy seeds that they are almost black. They mix them with sour cherries, cream cheese or apple to fill strudels and *biegli*, little Christmas pastries stuffed with a dense honey, walnut and poppy seed paste.

Stand in the covered market in Budapest and it's hard to believe Hungarians ever cook with anything other than their five grades of paprika. Bright strings of dried chillies fringe every stall and the powder – the colour of blood, bricks, rust and roses – comes in scarlet tins and little red-and-green cloth sacks.

It is thought paprika was brought to Hungary either by the Turks who occupied the country in the 17th century, or by ethnic groups from the Balkans, who were fleeing north from the Turks. Enchanted by the colour, Hungarian cooks started to experiment with paprika and discovered that, when meat is rubbed with it, then fried, it forms a crusty brown surface that mimics the effect of roasting meat over an open fire.

Juniper, that herby, bitter-sweet berry, makes me think of Christmas; perhaps it is the spiky bushes on which it grows. The small, purple-black berries thrive all over Northern Europe as well as the Mediterranean, and from France to Finland they are used in marinades for game, in terrines and sausages, and in après-ski braises of beef and venison. The Finns like a strong juniper flavour; they rub chickens with pine needles and handfuls of crushed juniper berries and leave them in the fridge for a couple of days to mature before roasting them. Juniper is lovely cooked with cabbage, the former's gin-like herbiness lending it a bit of sophistication.

Some familiar flavourings, such as ginger, allspice, cinnamon, cardamom and dill, can be seen in a new light when you look at how they're treated in cool climates. Dill, for example, is a comforting, non-assertive herb. Its name comes from the Norse *dilla*, meaning 'to lull', and it is the main ingredient in gripe water, the old-fashioned medicament for colicky babies. This herb brings a lovely snow-fresh feel to potato or fish gratins, braised or roast chicken, buttered carrots and dishes of onions, cabbages and beetroots. Use it in big handfuls and always add it at the end of cooking time. Or try caraway – once popular in Britain in breads, biscuits and cakes and now a signature flavouring in Austria, Hungary and Alsace – rubbed into roast pork or fried up with potatoes.

Soured cream speaks of Scandinavia and Eastern Europe more loudly than perhaps any other ingredient. It's thicker than regular cream and has a richness offset by acidity. It works in Scandinavian and Eastern European cooking either by complementing, or strongly contrasting with, other ingredients. Silky dill seems a natural partner for its clean flavour, but it's good too against the richness of smoked fish, the hot sweetness of paprika or the powderiness of floury potatoes. Scandinavians like simplicity in food and if you can make a sauce by stirring herbs or freshly grated horseradish into cream, they won't do anything more complicated.

Of course, Scandinavians and Eastern Europeans use soured cream just as much in the summer as in the winter, but I think of soured cream as a classic cold-weather ingredient, whispering of freshness and snow.

# 45

# THE MOON AND THE BONFIRES

Piedmont is famous for truffles and Barolo wine, but they're not the reason I went there. I read Cesare Pavese's *The Moon and the Bonfires* in my early thirties; it's not cheerful, but the Piedmontese landscape, almost a character in the novel, cures all ills and food connects everyone to it. Those who live there hold the place 'in their bones, like wine and polenta'. Pavese comes from Piedmont, from La Morra (a village I love). Like Seamus Heaney, he has his feet in the soil and his nose in the air. When I read, in one of his poems, 'the air's raw with fog, you drink it in sips like grappa,' I had to go. I like fog. I like those layers of mist hanging over vineyards you see in photographs of Piedmont.

In reality, it's more beautiful. I first went in October when there's a soothing stillness and the afternoons, especially if you're walking among fruit trees (there's lots of orchards and hazelnut groves, as well as vineyards), smell of mulch and apples so ripe they're almost fermenting.

The Piedmontese are taciturn, industrious, modest, the opposite of our stereotypical idea of Italians. The place feels well-heeled. Groups of middle-aged men, wearing thick jackets and soft scarves you want to stroke, sit outside bars drinking Barolo. It looks as if women get their hair done every week. When I had dinner there one New Year's Eve, a dog – beloved pet of the family at the next table – wore a pearl choker around her neck. The wine – specifically those from the nebbiolo grape (big, aromatic and reminiscent of tar, roses and wood smoke) – has brought money to the region, and wine and food and work are taken seriously. (I usually drink dolcetto, also from Piedmont; it's less expensive than Barolo, has a touch of bitterness and the dark lushness of black cherries.)

There are plenty of gourmet restaurants – Piedmont is regarded as one of the gastronomic centres of Italy – but I'm never looking for complicated stuff, and certainly not 'inventiveness'. One of the joys here is that you can take simple (if sometimes expensive) ingredients and turn them into unbelievable richness: partridges with wild mushrooms, *fonduta* – a cheese fondue made with egg yolks and milk – chocolate-stuffed pears baked in red wine. They love beef, butter, cream and cheese. Risotto and polenta are more common than pasta, though they do have their own thin egg pasta, *tajarin*. They use my favourite olive oil – the buttery stuff from Liguria – and, despite being landlocked, anchovies are a big deal.

Piedmont's position on the salt route, which winds its way from the sea at Liguria to the north, ensured that cured anchovies came to the area. Because of this, *bagna cauda*, an array of vegetables served with a bowl of anchovies melting to a purée in warm olive oil and butter (and piqued with garlic) is served everywhere. To have both anchovies and wild mushrooms in the same meal... that's some kind of heaven.

Then there's the nuts. At a small market one morning in La Morra, I tasted Piedmontese hazelnuts, and hazelnut paste, and the most exquisite hazelnut and chocolate spread. People will tell you where hazelnuts are best – Spain or France or Turkey – but you haven't tasted hazelnuts until you've tasted them here. Sweet and singing and intense, every hazelnut I eat is compared to the ones I can get in La Morra (and usually found lacking).

And then, of course, there are the truffles. I'd always been an inverted snob when it came to truffles. They were, I reasoned, out of the reach of most people, so I would just leave them. It's not that I don't believe in spending money on food, it's more that I'm suspicious of anything with a really high price tag, or that smacks of braggadocio and posturing. Were truffles really wonderful, or just a vehicle for bragging? Then I found myself, six years ago, sitting in an empty bar drinking a macchiato and waiting for my *trifolao*. Beppe, handsome, wild-haired, lots of useful pockets in his coat (which is what a truffle hunter needs), drove me to his special place with his equally wild-haired Lagotto, Luna.

Truffles are something of a miracle. A fruiting body of a fungus that grows underground, its web of filaments binds itself to the roots of trees, then feeds off it. In Piedmont, the trees that host truffles are oak, linden, hazel, poplar and beech and the white Alba truffles here are the most fragrant and sought after in the world. To fruit, they need the right degree of porosity in the soil around them, the right climate, the right amount of rainfall. Beppe and I scramble up and down small escarpments under trees, occasionally slipping on the damp ground. '*Vai, vai, Luna*!' he urges, making gentle clucking sounds that remind me of my dad coaxing horses. Luna starts to scrape frenziedly at the earth, busy with snout and paws. Beppe pulls her back firmly, giving her a biscuit (her reward), and strikes at the earth with a small pick until he pulls out a clod. Before the soil is brushed off you can smell it: beef, Parmesan, fungi, sweat, a briny seasidey whiff, like oysters... and sex. He hands me a truffle the size of a walnut and I breathe it in.

I'd scoffed at the idea of truffles being a drug, but I don't want to give it back. I close my eyes, breathe it in again. Now, wherever Luna runs, I'm right behind her. Even the faint scent – which you get as soon as the dog starts to paw at the ground – can be picked up quickly; my nose is attuned. Later, we study different sizes and types of white truffle. The most prized are as smooth as pebbles and spherical, others are lumpy. Red-tinged ones are from oaks; ivory specimens usually from poplars.

To experience them being shaved on to warm buttery *tajarin* is even better than that first scent on the hunt. The more a truffle's surface area is exposed to the air, the stronger the aroma; that's why you shave them thinly. The truffle falls in fine translucent slices, like damp slivers of air-dried ham or parchment, and I eat. On the rest of the trip I endeavour to be near truffles. Even if I'm not going to eat them – and I can't at every meal, they're too expensive – I sit by the truffle station in restaurants. This is usually a small table spread with a cloth, with a few scented nuggets sitting under a glass dome.

I had believed that once I'd seen the Northern Lights I could strike them off my list. It's not true, and it's not true of white truffles either. Both make you slightly mad with wonder. You simply want more. I don't buy truffles often, just once every couple of years, though I always eat them when I'm in Piedmont. A small truffle is the price of a pair of shoes, yes, but I'll forego other luxuries in order to have them. I crave them and think about them when

I'm not there, along with the hazelnuts, the walks among the apple trees, the *bagna cauda* and the Piedmontese fog. Not all addictions are bad; some are life-enriching.

# 46

# CARROTS AND CROWS

One of my earliest memories is of running in and out of our back garden, misty and smoky with the smell of coal fires, while my mother hung clothes on the washing line and chastised me for not eating my carrots. 'You see those big crows up there?' she'd ask. They were lined up, black-caped and evil-looking, cawing on the telephone wires. 'Well, they carry little girls away if they don't eat their carrots.' I had visions of being picked up by the shoulders of my cardigan and hoisted aloft, clinging to the plate of carrots that had wrought my demise.

It's amazing that I like carrots at all, given my crow experiences, but they're one of my favourite vegetables. I'd rather eat roast chicken with mashed potato and buttery carrots than almost anything else. I most often prepare them as they were at the spas at Vichy in France, mixed with butter, sugar and water, which evaporates during cooking. This method induces even my six-year-old to declare that he couldn't live without them.

Why do we despise winter vegetables, roots in particular? Maybe it's that unfortunate little quirk of human nature that makes us undervalue what is beneath our noses. Certainly our cold-weather vegetables provide more interesting and fitting dishes than the warm-climate interlopers flown halfway round the world to 'brighten' our darker months. Look at the colours for a start: the vivid orange of carrots, the magenta of beetroot, the mauve-tinged greenness of curly-leaved cabbages. I get as much pleasure out of dealing with these as I do from the more obviously glamorous spring and summer vegetables such as asparagus, peas and broad beans, but we also appreciate those because of their fleeting season. If King Edwards, with their soft, snowy flesh, were only available for six weeks in the year, we'd be cock-a-hoop about them, too.

Root vegetables bring sweet sustenance to a cold, grey world. Roasted, their sugars become so concentrated and caramelized that you have to push them with a spoon to dislodge their sticky bodies from the pan. They are easily as good as a plateful of roasted Mediterranean vegetables. And roasting is just the beginning. Carrots are good cooked with a splash of orange juice and a drizzle of honey, or simmered in stock and mixed with wild mushrooms and cream to make *carottes forestières*.

A classic candidate for roasting is the parsnip, a vegetable which British and American diners seem to be alone in liking. They can be roasted with brown sugar or maple syrup, or boiled, mashed with butter and cinnamon and crowned with a pile of sweet, browned onions. It is funny that the Russians have never really gone for the parsnip, given that the Russian word for them is *pasternak*. You'd think that a vegetable with the same name as the author of the romantic *Doctor Zhivago* would have a better image, but apparently not.

In Britain, we love potatoes, but we see them largely as mopper-uppers of other flavours; the support act, not the star. It's a pity when you think what can be done with them. The Savoie and Dauphiné regions of France have bubbling potato gratins; in the South-West they sauté them to an awesome richness in goose fat. In Italy they make gnocchi and croquettes from potatoes; Russians fry them with wild mushrooms. The Scandinavians, like the British, eat them at practically every meal, baking slices in dill-flavoured bechamel to serve with pork, for example. The Swiss and the Dutch cook them with pears and apples for just the same purpose. In Hungary and Austria, potatoes are sautéed with paprika and caraway, bathed in warm soured cream with nuggets of pickled cucumber, or mashed with curd cheese and chunks of speck. There's so much more to potatoes than mash and roasties.

Then there are the more recherché roots. Jerusalem artichokes, looking like knobbly potatoes wearing coats lent to them by root ginger, have melting, ivory-coloured flesh. They're good paired with salty or meaty ingredients: try them sliced and sautéed with bacon, black pudding or mushrooms, or use them to replace some of the potatoes in a gratin dauphinois, or to make a lovely tawny soup. They're the devil to peel, mind you, so I often don't. Flecks of beige in a soup or purée won't hurt anyone, and when roasted whole with little branches of thyme, the skin of a Jerusalem artichoke is as toothsome as the flesh.

Celeriac, a form of celery bred specially for its bulbous base, is also underused. Its celery flavour can be almost overwhelming and it needs strong foods such as game to stand up to it, but it's great tempered with potato and produces a mash with a real herby edge.

At one time I saw beetroot just as a salad ingredient pickled to within an inch of its life. Then I went to Scandinavia. One of the first meals I enjoyed in Sweden was a simple plate of hot-smoked trout, potatoes dressed with dill and soured cream and some globes of roasted beetroot, warm, crimson and still in their skins. What a partner they were for the salty smokiness of the fish, the aniseedy freshness of dill and the cold starkness of soured cream. I've also, in Denmark, had chopped beetroot mixed with capers to accompany cod with mustard sauce and, in Austria, eaten hot roast beetroot dressed with seasoned buttermilk alongside roast pork.

Russians and Poles love beetroot, too, using it in borscht and often as a partner for game, while Georgians grate and purée it to make salads and dips for their little mezze-style dishes, *zakuski*. If you don't cook beetroot, then try it: the colour is magnificent and its charms don't stop there.

It's a family joke that every time my father sits down to turnips he comments (always as if for the first time): 'It's a very underrated vegetable, turnip.' We all snigger, but I have to concur. Parboiled and fried with chunks of bacon, a good knob of butter and a shower of black pepper, it's surely worthy of more than feeding to pigs. Swede is even better – it is sweeter – though both do have a slight peppery bitterness which is perhaps an acquired taste.

School cabbage – the smell, the lack of seasoning, the bitter taste of the waterlogged slop that ends up on your plate – should put everyone off this vegetable for life. But there are so many stonking Eastern European cabbage dishes that, even if you think you hate it, you must give it another go. Crinkly, squeaky Savoy, shredded and cooked briskly in a tablespoon of water, a good knob of butter and flavourings such as crushed juniper, is a world away from the institutional stuff. In Hungary, I've had Savoy sautéed with onions and caraway; in Russia, baked with apples and soured cream; in Norway, sweated in butter with bacon and dill.

Red cabbage gets the classic fruit treatment in Britain and all over Eastern Europe, but it's also good with bacon, caraway, juniper and a dollop of soured cream, or with cranberries, pears or orange instead of the usual apple.

Purple-sprouting broccoli, another member of the cabbage family, appears in March and, though some regard it as a spring vegetable, I feel it is firmly placed earlier, at the brighter end of winter. While I never use it for anything complicated, I can't get enough. Its slender shape means that you can half-sauté and half-sweat it in olive oil and a splash of white wine: no full-scale steaming or boiling.

Despite the fact that vichyssoise is a summer soup, leeks are at their best from October to March and a pot of warm, creamy leek-and-potato soup is even better than its cold counterpart. This is a veg that, I'm afraid, is greatly enhanced by butter, and leeks do need to be softened in it to get the best out of them. Sweat shredded leeks in a covered pan with a splash of water and a good chunk of butter to serve with fish, or mix the softened veg with Savoy cabbage, drizzle with cream and bake under slices of melting fontina or Taleggio cheese. Leeks are often a good extra ingredient, perfuming the rest of a dish with a mild onion flavour: try layering them with potatoes and cheese in a cream- or stock-based gratin and you'll see what I mean. They make a great quiche-style tart too, especially if you spread a big spoonful of grain mustard into the pastry case before filling it.

Everywhere I went in snowy Northern Italy, I found radicchio, a vegetable I hadn't associated with cold weather. As well as the ubiquitous round *radicchio di Chioggia*, the one we most commonly see here, you're able to buy other varieties: *rosso di Verona*, with its small, tight round heads and slightly more delicate flavour; *rosso di Castelfranco*, a round rose-like variety; and *rossa di Treviso*, which resembles a little bush with long, quill-like leaves and broad ivory ribs. They all look spectacular, with their crimson-splattered creaminess. The Verona and Treviso varieties are great with nuts, pomegranates and smoked food, so find their way into winter salads. The various forms of radicchio are also sautéed or grilled and served as a side dish. This treatment softens their bitterness and turns their edges bronzed and wilting.

I also love the long, pale, bitter Belgian endive or chicory. Its flavour renders it truly wintry – that bite is like a cold gust of wind – and it's a great palate cleanser in a season when dishes are cooked to softness and sweetness. Left in *chicons*, it seems to last for ages in the bottom of the fridge and can be used in salads or braised in butter and bacon, maybe adding a little cream, or even in orange juice, for a side dish that offers something different.

Frisée, that mad, tangled mess of a lettuce, is another perfect choice for autumn and winter salads, especially those that contain apples, pears or cheese with a bit of bite, as its bitterness can take on strong flavours.

You think this cast of winter vegetables is dull? Absolutely not.

# 47

# CRIMSON LAKES

It is a freezing October in Massachusetts, and everywhere I look there are scarlet lakes surrounded by trees glowing with autumn foliage. The beauty of cranberries, Christmas-red and smooth as beads, ebbing and flowing in blue, flooded bogs, is mesmerizing. My eyes can barely cope with the colour. 'I love cranberry bogs when they're filled with water,' says Irene Sorenson. She looks after many of the cranberry farmers in this state, one of the biggest growing areas. 'They are so romantic: irregularly shaped, curvaceous, organic.'

Cranberry growers talk about their crop with love. Most of them are fifth or sixth generation and have berries in their blood. At this time of year, when the harvest is in full swing, they work around the clock. Some rest only by grabbing a bit of shut-eye under a tree in the woods near the bogs, but they will not leave their precious fruit.

In fact, most growers are so fond of cranberries that, despite their unalloyed tartness, you will see them throwing raw cranberries into the air and letting them fall into their mouths.

The cranberry is an ancient berry, indigenous to North America, and, since it formed part of the first Thanksgiving meal, a potent symbol of American beginnings and survival. It's certainly a plucky little berry. The naturally waxy coating will keep it fresh for a good three months in the bottom of the fridge and it's cute and endlessly cheering, too. The native Americans ate cranberries fresh and used them in *pemmican*, a kind of energy bar made with preserved venison and fat. They also used the juice to dye blankets and feathers and made poultices from them, while a basket of cranberries often sat in the middle of meetings with different tribes, as a sign of friendship and goodwill.

When you look at the stacks of cranberries that arrive in our shops every Christmas, it's hard to believe they haven't always been this abundant, but at one time they only grew wild. People picked them from patches near their homes, just for themselves. Commercial cultivation only started two centuries ago and the berries were harvested 'dry', picked with long wooden combs. It was a slow and back-breaking process. Nowadays, most are harvested 'wet'. The bogs where they grow are flooded and large machines with big whirling arms – referred to as 'egg beaters' – are driven through, gently dislodging berries from the vines. Because they contain little air pockets, they float to the surface of the water. They are then corralled towards a pipe, in pools marbled in shades of crimson and salmon-pink. As most are destined for juice or sauce it doesn't matter that they get so wet, but fruit to be sold fresh is still dry-harvested, collected by machines that look like large lawn mowers.

Sadly, cranberries suffer from being part of our Christmas. Once the decorations are down, we don't think about them until the next December. It's a crying shame, especially when our winter fruits are so limited. We could do with cranberry's tartness and piercing colour right through into the spring. They'll certainly keep that long, providing stunning sorbets and bringing bursts of flavour and brightness to crumbles, cobblers, bread-and-butter puddings, tarts, cakes and compotes (they are spectacular gently poached in sugar syrup, mixed with blood orange slices).

I don't just use these berries for puddings. Cranberry sauce is great with pork. Many of the cranberry pickers in Massachusetts are of Cape Verdean origin and celebrate the end of the harvest with a hog roast accompanied by cranberry sauce. It also makes a fine substitute for the lingonberry sauce that is eaten with Scandinavian meat dishes, and it's easier to make, since fresh lingonberries are difficult to get hold of here.

Cranberries are a must for Russian cooking, too. There they are made into *kissel* (a fruit compote thickened with arrowroot), find their way into tarts, are steeped in vodka to make cranberry liqueur or mashed with horseradish to make a relish for beef. And the Finns love them. You can see them in the market in Helsinki, bobbing in barrels of water alongside the smaller lingonberries. Dried cranberries, always slightly sweetened, are available all year round and they're perfect for bringing little nuggets of sweet-sour flavour to wild rice salads.

So the cranberry isn't just for Christmas. Buy them, freeze them or stash them somewhere cool and enjoy their tart fruitiness right up until the winter ends.

In England, blackberries are regarded as a fruit of the late summer and early autumn. But, growing up in Northern Ireland, I thought of blackberry picking as an activity for October and a definite sign that autumn was in full swing. There were still plenty of blackberries in the hedgerows, even after the clocks had gone back. I remember coming home in the near-dark, as layers of mist settled over the fields, with saucepans and milk cans full of them. With hands scratched and stained, we cooked the fruit immediately. Looking at their glossy black bodies, it was hard to believe they wouldn't remain intact and beautiful but, as the poet Seamus Heaney reminds us, they don't keep. A fur starts to creep over them, he writes: 'A rat-grey fungus, glutting on our cache.' Any hope that they would survive would be bludgeoned the next day... and you were left with a gnawing guilt that you had taken more fruit than you needed.

To enjoy blackberries, you need to pick them yourself. Those in the shops are expensive, relatively tasteless, and, anyway, blackberries are best appreciated when you have so many you don't know what to do with them. All sweet and black and free, the abundance makes your head spin.

Blackberries are widely cultivated in the United States, where the berries grow on erect, woody plants rather than sprawling brambles. They make so many of their great desserts with them – cobblers and buckles and slumps – that they certainly need them. A 'black-and-blue' cobbler, made with blackberries and blueberries and covered with a biscuity buttermilk dough, may sound homely, but, with its network of crimson juices bursting through pastry, is wickedly alive.

Blackberries are popular in Eastern Europe and through the Caucasus as well, though more as an accompaniment to meat than as a dessert. Georgians use them for their famous tart sauces, pushing the puréed fruit through a sieve before mixing it with garlic and chilli, dill and coriander, a great accompaniment to lamb kebabs or roast chicken, though I prefer to add a little sugar, too.

A simple treatment is best for blackberries. Eat them in apple and blackberry tarts, crumbles made with brown sugar and chunks of hazelnuts and walnuts, or just on their own with some clotted cream and a sprinkling of sugar. English food writer Dorothy Hartley suggests a blackberry salad made by leaving the berries somewhere warm and then adding sugar and red wine just before serving, and they make a lovely autumn fruit salad with chunks of ripe melon and a ginger syrup.

I think of rosehips as the strawberries of autumn. Not that you can scoff them in the same carefree way – the seeds of the hip are covered with tiny hairs – it's just that they carry the taste of strawberries and roses. I started looking for good places to pick rosehips because I yearned to recapture the flavour of the rosehip syrup that my grandmother kept. It wasn't such an unusual foodstuff to have around in her day. Rosehips are so full of vitamin C that, during the Second World War, children were sent to gather them to make syrup. This syrup was given as a vitamin supplement and you can still buy it in some pharmacies.

When I first visited Scandinavia, I was amazed to see how mainstream rosehips were there. In Sweden, rosehip juice is as prominent on shop shelves as orange juice. In winter, this is heated to make a warm, sweet soup, while whole rosehips are added to pear and apple tarts. The Russians and Poles love these little berries, too, principally as a jelly to eat with game. I like the jelly with venison, as a topping for warm scones and to melt into warm rice pudding, or in a salad of speck and prosciutto with peppery leaves. It was a dollop of rosehip jelly I had in Northern Italy that made me realize how good it was with charcuterie.

Gather rosehips after they've been softened by the first frosts, usually around the end of October, and use them soon after picking. To make rosehip jelly, just cook washed ripe rosehips with twice their weight in cooking apples in enough water to cover. When the fruit is soft and pulpy – it will take about forty-five minutes – put it in a jelly bag and let it drip overnight. Put the extracted juice in a large saucepan and add 450g (1lb) sugar for every 568ml (1 pint) of juice. Heat gently until the sugar has dissolved, then boil rapidly for fifteen minutes, or until the setting point is reached – put 1 teaspoon of the hot liquid on a chilled saucer and see whether it wrinkles when you push it with your finger – then pot in sterilized jars.

Sloes are perhaps the hardest of autumn berries to like. Mouth-puckeringly astringent, they are not for straightforward eating, but for steeping in gin or vodka with sugar. My uncle used to turn up with a bottle of his sloe gin every year just before Christmas and we hoarded it as though it was vintage Champagne. Tasting of Ribena and clove rock sweets, it was the first alcohol I ever liked.

Now you can buy commercially made versions, but for some reason they taste medicinal; it is much better to make your own. And don't just keep it for Christmas. Added to Champagne, it makes a wonderful British-style kir, while the boozy little bodies left behind after you've strained off the gin can be incorporated into a chocolate truffle mix: a treat for the greedy cook.

# 48

# RIPE AND READY

Cheese-making may be simple in theory – a starter culture makes milk coagulate into curds, which are then pressed – but think of the textures and flavours on offer: a precipice of crumbling Parmesan; a ripe snowy Camembert, its insides full to bursting; Époisses, pungent and supple with an orange rind that sticks to your fingers. These differences are the result of all the variables that can affect a cheese: what milk is used, whether the animal has grazed on grass or hay, whether the ground is clay or limestone, volcanic or granite, the way a cheese coagulates and its curds are cut and pressed, the salting method used, the length and place of curing.

It's amazing to think that most cheeses are the result of centuries of farmers and dairymen playing with chance, imagination and their tastebuds. And it all comes from one simple ingredient: milk, the primal food of every mammal.

Cheese is one of the best cold-weather foods and some cheeses seem made for winter. Cooked cheese – melting, warm and creamy – gives both comfort and central heating to our bodies. For years, I stayed every winter in a little family-run hotel in the Haute-Savoie. Here, the cheese trolley was the crowning glory of every meal. *'Vous avez choisi, Madame?'* the owner would ask me every night. He knew that, faced with two tiers of cheeses from the Savoie and the Jura in peak condition, I didn't want to choose at all. I wanted the whole damned lot.

The restaurant here showed me that the joys of cooked Alpine cheeses weren't limited to fondue. Tartiflette, a Savoyard dish of potatoes and onions topped with a creamy blanket of melting Reblochon, is one of the most satisfying dishes I know. Add the traditional accompaniments of salami, little sweet-and-sour onions, cornichons and a green salad and you wonder why you ever bother to cook anything fancier. Then there's pumpkin or onion soup smothered in molten Gruyère, or raclette, an ancient mountain cheese made in the French Savoie and the Valais region of Switzerland. Once heated on a grill, it becomes sweetly savoury and wonderfully elastic, perfect for scooping up with bread or warm waxy potatoes.

In the Italian Dolomites, you find pasta with pumpkin and nuggets of smoked ricotta, while in Italy's Valle d'Aosta there is a soup made up of layers of bread, greens and supple fontina, all collapsing in the warmth of chicken broth. In the cold of a Normandy winter, you find Camembert soaked in Calvados and baked. Alsace offers little toasts covered with melting spicy Munster served with plum compote or toasted cumin seeds, while Piedmont has risottos so dripping with Taleggio that they're best eaten with a spoon. Britain has Welsh rarebit, tarts stuffed with smoked fish and mature Cheddar and deep bowls of cauliflower soup scattered with salty Stilton.

In these dishes, cheese is the star, though there are plenty of others in which it is an enhancer, blending well with another distinct ingredient: pork chops topped with a layer of ham and Gruyère; rare steak dotted with Roquefort butter; a gratin of haddock, mussels and spinach baked with Cheddar.

And you don't have to cook much to make cheese into lunch or supper. Want an effortless end to a wintry meal? Serve damson or quince cheese with a wedge of Stilton or Lanark Blue; offer Gorgonzola and mascarpone with drizzles of honey and freshly shelled walnuts, or with pears poached in spiced red wine; give guests apples with a hunk of Montgomery Cheddar and cobnuts.

Some cheeses – such as Cheddar, Gorgonzola and Camembert, for example – seem right for eating all year round, but there are others with a particularly wintry appeal. Those from the French, Swiss and Italian Alps, not surprisingly, hit the spot. Put the Savoyard Beaufort at the top of your list. Floral, milky and herbal, it is the supreme Gruyère-type cheese and worth more than just grating into a fondue: it makes a wonderful tart, with ham and nutmeg, and is great in *gougères*, too. Other good elastic melting cheeses, though all of them less aromatic than Beaufort, are Comté, Emmental and Gruyère. Look out, too, for Tomme de Savoie, an ancient French mountain cheese made in the winter, with a gentle taste of meadows.

Semi-soft Morbier, from the Jura, is sweet and fruity with a yeasty smell and a layer of ash through the middle. It's such a good melter that a wheel of it would traditionally be set up near the fire and scraped off on to bread or hot potatoes as it started to soften. Reblochon, used to make tartiflette, is a semi-soft washed rind cheese with a farmyardy smell, yet a taste of walnuts and flowers. Vacherin Mont d'Or is gloriously fruity, smooth and runny. Baked in its wooden box until the crust becomes golden, it makes a great meal for two; like a fondue but without the hassle. Taleggio, a great grilling cheese from Lombardy (try it over hot polenta), has a rusty-hued crust and a melting curd which smells of almonds and hay. Fontina, a smooth elastic cheese from the Valle d'Aosta, tastes of mushrooms and is used for the Italian-style fondue dish, *fonduta*.

Blue cheeses are great with autumn fruits, nuts and bitter winter leaves such as chicory; try dense Fourme d'Ambert from the Auvergne in South-West France, or mild Bleu du Haut-Jura (also known as Bleu de Gex), as well as clean, crumbly Roquefort.

Sadly, too many Scandinavian cheeses are made by big cooperatives rather than small artisans, but it's worth searching out the Swedish Herrgårdsost – fresh, tangy and Gruyère-like – and Danish Samsø, with its tiny holes and pungent sweet-sour flavour. Norwegian gjetost, a sweet cheese made from whey, is delicious with pickles and ham and is often used to make a sauce to go with game, especially venison. It's not to everyone's taste – when I say it's fudgy, I mean it – but it's distinctive and everyone should try it once.

All this makes cheese shopping – trying to choose between all those turrets and wheels and neat little boxes – one of the most pleasurable activities I know. Use the cold months to track down a good cheese shop and see what the snowy regions of the world have to offer.

# 49

# MARMALADE

It's almost risky giving a recipe for marmalade. It is the preserve most likely to get people hot under the collar. Some marmalade-makers don't make any other preserves; marmalade is their thing. And it's not just a preserve, it's an annual project, undertaken in the dark days of winter when the kingly Seville orange reaches our shores. Kitchens are filled with citrus smells – from the first nose-pricking spray that comes from the zest, to the rich, deep scent of cooked peel, juice and sugar – for days on end. Each cook's booty, whether it is pale with fine shreds or thick, chunky and dark, is the only marmalade which that particular cook rates.

Modern marmalade, however you like it, is quite different from the form it first took. A fruit conserve known as *marmelada* started being shipped to Britain from Portugal in the 15th century. But it hadn't been anywhere near an orange. It got its name from the fruit on which it was based, the *marmelo*, the Portuguese word for quince. Britain already had recipes for quince preserves, but this was different. It was a firm paste that came in pretty boxes (some were even set in fancy moulds) and it still exists in Portugal, though most people in Britain are probably more familiar with its Spanish counterpart, membrillo. C Anne Wilson, in her thorough history of marmalade, thinks that Portuguese *marmelada* was probably flavoured with flower water, which would have made it exotic and different.

Gradually, 'marmalade' became the general name for fruit pastes and preserves (there are recipes in 16th-century cookbooks for apple and pear 'marmalades'), but it's difficult to know how or when marmalade became a preserve made only from citrus fruits. The recipe book of a Madam Eliza Cholmondeley (dated around 1677) has one of the first English recipes for citrus marmalade that we know of. Her 'Marmalet of Oranges' would produce a very thick dark substance, almost as firm as *marmelada*. Some fifty years later, Mary Kettilby, in her book *A Collection of Above Three Hundred Receipts in Cookery, Physick and Surgery*, gives a marmalade recipe that instructs us to 'boil the whole pretty fast until it will jelly'. A jelly with peel suspended in it? Sounds like the stuff I have in my cupboard.

It's the Scots who are credited with developing marmalade as a spread, and certainly Scottish recipes of the mid-18th century used more water, producing a less solid-set preserve.

When sugar became cheaper in the latter half of the 19th century, commercial jam-making really took off. Marmalade was perfect for winter production, though it was initially a luxury item exported to British homes throughout the Empire. It was the Scots who democratized it, making it affordable to all classes and the bitter-sweet stalwart of the British breakfast table.

I risk the ire of marmalade-makers everywhere, but I'm rather partial to the soft-set orange blossom-laced stuff. Marmalade? Well, it wouldn't be served at a sensible Scottish breakfast. It's Middle Eastern, rather syrupy and doesn't stay on your toast. But there are days when the chunky dark stuff seems a bit stern. And in the vast panoply of citrus preserves that take the moniker 'marmalade' today, one that harks back to its scented beginnings seems rather apt.

50

# SUGAR SNOW

'How will I know which are the sugar houses?' I ask my friend Ed, a native Vermonter. 'Oh, you'll know!' he laughed. 'They're the ones that look like they're on fire.' And indeed, all over the Vermont countryside were wooden cabins, some little more than shacks, with huge clouds of smoke billowing from their roofs. I was in Vermont for the sugaring season, when sugar-makers tap the maple tree sap and make their maple syrup.

Driving in from Boston the night before, I'd caught my first sight of the galvanized collecting buckets hanging from the maple trees, lit by the moon reflecting off the surface of the snow. The practice looked even more pure and old-fashioned than I had imagined, and I'd been waiting thirty years to see it. On autumn afternoons when I was growing up in Northern Ireland, my teacher had read us Laura Ingalls Wilder's *Little House* books, about the life of a family of settlers in the late 19th century in Wisconsin. I had shared Mary and Laura's excitement as a 'sugar snow' developed; the kind of snow that indicates the right conditions for tapping the sap. Later, their grandparents held a sugar-on-snow party, when the syrup was boiled up, then poured on to clean snow, where it set in cobwebs of maple toffee. The idea of Americans still making sugar-on-snow like this seemed perhaps a tad fanciful, but on my trip I soon saw notices for community sugar-on-snow parties, where there would be warm cider, baked ham and potatoes, maple-baked beans, doughnuts, sugar-on-snow and dill pickles. (Dill pickles are the archetypal accompaniment to sugar-on-snow, cleansing your palate before you take the next mouthful of toffeed maple.)

The russet colour of maple syrup makes you think of it as the quintessential autumn ingredient, but it's actually made in February and March. Native Americans, who were the first to make it, used to watch for the 'sugar moon', the first sign that it was time to tap the trees. They boiled the sap right down, further than syrup, until it turned to granular sugar that was easier to store, and for a long time it was the only form of sweetener available. There weren't many beekeepers to provide honey and, although molasses from the West Indies sugar plantations became plentiful, it was pretty much boycotted by New Englanders, because the trade in molasses supported slavery in the most direct way. 'Make your own sugar and send not to the Indies for it,' advised the *Farmers' Almanac* in 1803. 'Feast not on the toil, pain and misery of the wretched.'

Willis Wood, a handsome bear of a man and a sugar-maker for almost thirty years, is wrapped in layers of jerseys and clasps a warm mug of coffee. As it's the height of the sugaring season, he's boiling sap almost twenty-four hours a day, starting early, finishing late and practically sleeping in his snowbound cabin. He sniffs the air, trying to ascertain if the sap will flow today. Maple sap will only flow when it both freezes at night and rises above freezing during the day, so you never know what will happen. About two hundred gallons of sap come into his sugar house every hour, but, as it takes forty gallons to make a single gallon of maple syrup, he needs it all.

Willis tells me that, though the process of making syrup has become more efficient, the basic transformation of sap into syrup by boiling it down hasn't changed. 'The sap itself looks just like water and isn't even slightly syrupy. It's amazing that anyone discovered what could be done with it,' he says. 'Trees generally have no more than three taps – more than that puts the tree under stress – these days made by electric drills. Into these we put spouts and the sap runs through them into buckets.' Small-time sugarers – and there are plenty of 'mom-and-pop' operators who manage to make enough to sell syrup commercially –

and all 'backyard' sugarers, who do it just for fun, collect their sap in this way, using buckets, but for more commercial enterprises, plastic tubing has come in big time. Squirrels and moose can gnaw through this, so it isn't completely efficient, but it cuts down on labour as nobody has to go and collect all those buckets, the vacuum system pumps out six times more sap than conventional taps and the tubing carries the syrup directly to the sugar house.

Once here, the graft of making the syrup begins in earnest. Willis boils the sap in a large metal trough over a huge wood-fuelled fire. He stokes the fire every seven minutes and stirs the syrup, waiting for it to get to that optimum point when enough water has been boiled away and the syrup is ready to be drawn off. Judging this is initially done by eye. Willis scoops the syrup up on a wide paddle and lets it drip, waiting to see if it is thick enough to 'apron' or spread out in a wide, amber sheet. At this point, the process is usually completed in a finishing pan, where the sugarer can keep a closer eye on the temperature, then the syrup is filtered and bottled while still warm. It's a labour of love and produces that rare thing nowadays: a totally unadulterated food.

All this would just be romantic if it didn't also produce a fantastic ingredient. I didn't just fall in love with the idea of maple syrup early in life, I fell in love with its flavour, too, starting by pouring dark pools of it on to pancakes, then on to sautéed apples to go with ice cream and into pans of fudge. Used in nut-based cakes, for both the batter and the frosting, maple syrup enhances the flavour of pecans, walnuts and hazelnuts, and seems to make cakes that are particularly good for eating with a mug of coffee.

I now also use maple syrup in savoury dishes, for example for making glazes – perhaps along with whisky, mustard or chilli – to brush on roast pork, chicken or sausages. In fact, it goes really well with all the ingredients we associate with autumn and winter: pork, apples and pears, nuts and pumpkin (try drizzling a little maple syrup on wedges of pumpkin for roasting).

Maple syrup varies in flavour – the palest having the lightest taste, the darkest having the strongest – and its flavour is pretty much as you would expect if you look at maple leaves: toasted and reminiscent of burnt sugar and fudge. It makes the flavour of sugar seem dead and one-dimensional in comparison. I generally use the darkest syrup I can get my hands on: it has the deepest, most maple-y flavour.

Before I left Vermont, I got to have my Laura Ingalls Wilder experience, attending a sugar-on-snow party with a hundred or so school kids. There were no dill pickles, but as we dived on to the maple toffee left by a barrel on wheels (a clever contraption designed by local sugar-makers) we really didn't care.

51

# BACK HOME

It's hard for me to listen to Van Morrison's song 'Coney Island'. It's not about Coney Island in New York, but about a little island in Lough Neagh in Northern Ireland. It relays the small details of a Sunday driving round that area in autumn sunshine, picking up the Sunday papers, doing a bit of bird-watching. As Van says, 'the craic was good.' The line which gets me is this: 'Stop off at Ardglass for a couple of jars of mussels and some potted herrings, in case we get famished before dinner.' Van growls through this – half-singing, half-speaking – in his untouched Northern Irish accent. And there is my father, summed up in a song.

Most years we went to Dublin on holiday, and the first stopping point was a place where Dad bought cockles and mussels. He ate them in the car, from little paper cartons. The shellfish stop indicated that we were really on our holidays, that we were going to the Republic of Ireland, and that dad was happy. Food marked this holiday excitement, but also a joy taken in life. 'Here, try it!' he would often command, holding out a forkful of some new flavour and texture, willing us to be more adventurous.

My dad is only seventy-eight – not old – but I know that one day I will listen to 'Coney Island' and that it will be unbearable.

My mum was the cook in our family. I am of the generation when that was a mother's job. When Dad cooked – flipping marinated chicken thighs on the barbecue, messing up the entire kitchen making chicken liver pâté – it stood out, it was something special. It seems unfair, therefore, that my dad's attitude to and love for food influenced me perhaps even more than my mum's... but it did.

When he went away on a trip, it was always food he brought back: jars of Scandinavian herrings, shining silver behind glass, bought hurriedly at airport duty-free; links of fat sausages from Buckley's in Dublin, which he would triumphantly produce from his briefcase (we always had those on Christmas morning); silky smoked salmon. He picked up wild stuff, too, from friends. Big salmon – so fresh they looked as if they might still leap – and pheasants in the feather (though I hated those, with their beady eyes and soft, small-boned bodies).

When we went on our first foreign holiday – to Portugal – we had one night in a 'posh' restaurant. The rest of us ordered dishes we recognized. Dad ordered salt cod fritters and cataplana. We marvelled at this big copper spaceship of pork and clams (what an odd combination, what a dish), which he emptied, tackling every last clam with his big hands. At every turn, he urged us to try the new, the unusual. I know that my dad's love of food really formed me. From my mother, I learned skills. From my father, I learned to taste the world.

# 52

# MISSING NEW YORK

It's 1968 and I'm sitting on a rug in the garden. My mum is reading from one of the American books we got free with our new set of *Collier's Encyclopedia*. Every time she finishes the story of 'Rosa Too Little', I beg her to read it again. I want it over and over.

Rosa lives in a brownstone in New York and her family can't afford books (never mind a set of encyclopedias) and she's too little to join the library. Instead, she plays in the bright sprays of water that gush from the fire hydrants on hot days. By the end of the story, Rosa joins the library and can have as many books as she wants. She is Rosa Too Little no longer. I was waiting to join the library too and, because of Rosa, I knew it was going to happen. I also – because I wanted to be there, dancing in the water, then sitting on the stoop with Rosa – fell in love with New York.

I'm not the only one. New York is a nexus of lights and hope. We feel we know it even if we've never been. Irish people have always been drawn there, because of famine or poverty or simple optimism. In the early 1860s, one in every four New Yorkers was an Irish immigrant. I grew up in a different time in Irish history but I knew, early on (the Troubles started in the late 1960s), that I would have to leave Northern Ireland. Home was never really home. I was only going to be there for a little while. I played 'Rhapsody in Blue' – one of only ten LPs we had – and fed my fantasy with books (a Canadian aunt sent picture books in which children ate cookies the size of the moon and shopped in dime stores). I wanted to be in New York.

By the age of eleven, I thought I could be Rhoda, the star of the American sitcom (even though I was neither Jewish nor from the Bronx). She was just so sassy. We lived in the middle of the countryside, but, at night, I would look out of the landing window at the lights across the fields. It was actually the glow of the nearby housing estate – and the small row of shops where we sometimes picked up groceries – but no matter. With a determined imagination and the right music, it was the sparkling edges of Manhattan.

Even going to Dublin got me that bit nearer. When we went there on holidays we always visited the airport, not to fly somewhere, but to experience the possibility of flying somewhere. The departures board was intoxicating. 'Bong bing, Aer Lingus!' my siblings and I would say, imitating the finest Dublin accent, then laugh ourselves silly. We watched the big white-and-green birds with shamrocks on their sides take off for Boston and Chicago and New York. You see? New York wasn't far away. But I only got there in stages.

New York is a fantasy and the first few times you visit that's all you see. Walk/Don't Walk signs, plumes of steam rising from manhole covers, skyscraper restaurants from where you can view the whole glittering grid of the city, surly bartenders who say 'Whaddya want?' It's a movie made real, and you run your own narrative and images. The thing that made me happiest, on my first visit, was that the Empire State Building wasn't swanky. It was nearly Christmas and the pots of poinsettia in the lobby were covered in old crinkled aluminium foil. I thought it was exactly as it would have looked if I'd visited with Rosa in 1968.

I wanted to watch the skating at the Rockefeller Centre, look down the central spine of the Guggenheim, see Jasper Johns's *Flag* at The Museum of Modern Art, but most of my plans centred around food. The hot dog carts, the red sauce Italians, the little cardboard cartons of Chinese takeout; these were as much a part of New York as the Statue of Liberty. For a long time, I'd been looking at what New York chefs were cooking and I chose my restaurants carefully. Two of them – Annie Rosenzweig's Arcadia and Danny Meyer's Union Square Café – remained favourites for years. I explored simple neighbourhood joints, too. I wanted a diner I could call my own. 'Can you speak Spanish?' drawled the waiter in one place (as I tried to eat a sandwich as big as my head). 'Why?' 'Because this dude doesn't speak English and I'm havin' trouble here.' So I took the order from the man from Venezuela – feeling like a native – and understood that eating in New York wasn't just about food, but about interaction. I returned from that first trip with a tortilla press from Zabar's (you can forget Dean & Deluca and all the fancy-pants delis, I wanted to go to places that were chaotic and scuffed at the edges) and a notebook full of ideas, not for books or columns (I wasn't a food writer then), but for my own kitchen.

I look to New York for shots of culinary energy. When I'm at home in London, I enjoy it vicariously by checking out the menus of favourite restaurants online, and every week I wait for the 'Hungry City' column in *The New York Times*. It doesn't cover smart places, but small inexpensive out-of-the way ones: an Uzbek restaurant where the *plov* is splattered with barberries and black cumin; a Mexican joint where the margaritas sting and English is understood, though not spoken. I could never eat my way round all these – even if I lived there – but the column offers vignettes and moods, a picture of the world that has washed up on New York's shore; life, through food, in the Naked City.

When I'm in New York, I'm up and out of my hotel – breakfast being the first great meal of the day there – by 7.30am. In late spring and summer, the city smells of hot pavements (even better when they're hot and wet, then you can get a whiff of blossom in some neighbourhoods) and food: garlicky pizza, hot sugar-dusted doughnuts, salty pretzels. Each day has a schedule: I visit cheese shops, bakeries and tea houses, places that specialize in Indian breakfasts and Cantonese desserts. I eat oysters and steak and knock back Manhattans. I watch how much pleasure others take in food, like the Japanese man in a cagoule, standing at a counter by himself eating crab in one of the city's food markets, his face creased with concentration.

Odd places – such as the Italian where I can get eggs and anchovies on toast for breakfast and the best chocolate and hazelnut cake I've ever tasted – have become regular haunts. Some of the most enjoyable finds aren't planned, like the Irish bar I discovered at 3am. Run by two Dubliners, it's a refuge for chefs who've just finished their shifts. The burgers aren't remarkable, but the high-energy exhaustion is. And everyone has a tale to tell, even if you can work it out without hearing it.

On every trip, I make a pilgrimage to 97 Orchard Street on the Lower East Side. It's a museum, but not a place of glass cases and dead history. It's in an old tenement building where immigrants lived and the apartments – each representing a different family and era – tell the story of what they did and how they ate. I partly go there to be reminded of New York's beginnings and the people who made this city, but also because it's a good area for eating. Even though it's increasingly gentrified, you can still find the food of those who came and wanted the comfort of the flavours they'd left behind: the Germans, Italians, East European Jews, Chinese and West Indians. You can still get bialys at Kossar's, lox at Russ & Daughters and pastrami on rye at Katz's Deli. And you should. New York is still peopled by the rest of the world. One-third of the inhabitants were born elsewhere and half speak a language other than English at home.

This means it's a compression of histories and dishes people hold on to, and which you can taste, too. It's not only the edible history or the culinary diversity that seduces, though, it's the glamour. Restaurateurs here don't just create places to eat. Go to Minetta Tavern, a 1930s Greenwich Village relic that was buffed, restored and opened in 2009. Pull back the heavy velvet curtain behind the door and you enter a complete world, a clubby, buzzing stage set filled with real people. You're Alice, falling down the rabbit hole. *The New York Times*'s restaurant critic, Pete Wells, has said that the city is brilliant at artifice; restaurateurs here are like theatre producers. They're good at making the new feel old, too. Take a cab across the Brooklyn Bridge – a ride, as you look at the skylines on both sides of the Hudson, that most makes you feel fused with the city – and head for Maison Premiere, a restaurant, oyster house and, as the owners describe it, 'cocktail den'. It looks pleasingly worn; laughter and noise spill on to the pavement. A small garden at the back is full of tumbling vines and a thousand fairy lights. It feels like New York, New Orleans and Paris all rolled into one and has the confidence of a long-established haunt, but it's only been there since 2011. It takes a city with chutzpah to pull that off.

Small town girls, like me, lack cynicism and aren't prone to ennui. We're lucky. For us, a place like New York is a constant source of wonder. I make a note of places I see from buses and taxis. What does Papaya Dog sell, or the (open twenty-four hours) Alaska Food Market? What is lunch like at the God Bless Deli? What is more exciting than driving past block after block of neon signs that light up the most intriguing-looking dining destinations and wondering what stories you'll find there?

I know New York isn't perfect. It's loud, it can be brash, people are too concerned with money. But it's also misrepresented. New Yorkers are frank rather than rude, friendly rather than in-your-face. A complete stranger will tell you that the novel you're reading isn't 'all that'; another will want to know what you paid for your handbag. You can be anonymous here, but it's unlikely people will let you.

Somehow I never got the apartment where my Chinese food could be delivered, where I would set my paper bag of groceries on the counter and wonder what to cook. I got waylaid by other things. But it's never too late to have a New York kitchen. Everything is possible...

# INDEX

**A**
*achar* 168–9
Acton, Eliza 167
Adrià, Ferran 32
*aglio e olio* 21
Agnes 115, 116
aïoli 24
al-Mushafi, Shafer ben Utman 209
Alexander, Stephanie 175–6
allioli 24, 32
allspice 45, 259
Amalfi 109
anchovies 57, 59–61
Andalusia 31, 37, 160
Andoh, Elizabeth 195
Andrews, Colman 58
Antony, Mark 45, 90
*apéritif* 177–9
apples 197–200, 201, 202
Arabs 36, 92, 113, 211–12
Arcadia 306
*arroz negro* 32, 33
Austria 172, 256, 271
autumn 163, 216–18, 223–6

**B**
bacon 231
*bagna cauda* 263
basil 155, 156–7, 161–2
Basques 30, 58

beans 233–7
Beauvoir, Simone de 120
Bedouin tribes 45, 211
beetroot 270–1
Belgian endive 273
Belgium 225
Beppe 264
Bilson, Gay 138–9
blackberries 216, 278–80
Books for Cooks 125
*boorani* 83
Bordeaux 71–2
borlotti (cranberry) beans 235
bottarga 61
bread 133–4, 140, 186–92
　　crumbs 133–4
　　flatbreads 185–92
　　toast 129–31
Britain 240, 242, 259, 285
　　apples 197–8
　　bread and toast 129, 130, 133
　　chutneys and pickles 166, 168
　　marmalade 289–90, 291
　　vegetables 269, 272
Brittany 74, 75
broom buds 166
Browning, Frank 198
Bunyard, Edward 173
burrata 112–13
butter beans 235

# INDEX

**C**
cabbage 271–2
cakes 39
Callas, Maria 106, 107
Canetti, Elias 186
cannellini beans 234–5
caraway 256, 259
cardamom 43, 44–5, 91, 93, 256, 259
carrots 267–8
cassoulet 233, 237, 247
Catalonia 30, 32, 59
cayenne pepper 47
celeriac 270
ceps 242–3
Chabrol, Claude 73
chanterelles 243
cheese 85–6, 140, 283–7
    burrata 112–13
    feta 156–8
    ricotta 86–7, 113
chermoula 158
chestnuts 252–3
Chez Panisse 123–5, 126, 127, 137
chicken 143–5, 152, 203
chicory 273
chillies 47–8, 100, 183, 258
Cholmondeley, Madam Eliza 290
Christ 37
chutneys 165–70, 173
cinnamon 45–6, 47, 91, 259
Çiya Sofrası 99
Clarke, Sally 137
Clarke's 137
Cleopatra 44–5, 90
Clothilde 19, 25–6, 72, 73
cobblers 279
cod 58–9
coffee 45
Cohen, Leonard 36
Coney Island, Lough Neagh 299, 300
Copenhagen 255–6
Cordon Bleu 136
coriander 43, 156, 158, 159, 161
coriander seeds 49
corn 163–4, 183
Costanzo, Corrado 113
cranberries 275–8
cravings 57–61
'crazy water' 15

cream 138
*cremat* 33
crudités 139
crumbles 280
crumbs 133–4
cumin 43, 47, 48–9, 91

**D**
Dağdeviren, Musa 99
damsons 171, 173–4
Daniel 71
dates 207, 211–12
David, Elizabeth 65
Denmark 174, 270
dill 157–8, 255, 256, 259
dinner parties 136–7, 141–2
Dordogne 245, 250
Dublin 299, 300, 304–5
dukka 48
Durand, Joël 64

**E**
East India Company 166
Ed 293
eggs 77–9
Egypt 41, 48, 187–8
Evelyn, John 166

**F**
fattoush 158
Fearnley-Whittingstall, Hugh 144
feta-type cheeses 85–6, 87, 156–8
figs 175, 207–9
Finland 258, 278
fish 57–61, 300
flageolet beans 235
flatbreads 185–92
flowers 89–95
focaccia 64, 186, 187, 188
France 16, 28, 63, 81, 141, 245–8
    *apéritif* 177–8
    apples 198
    beans 233, 234
    cheese 284, 285–7
    falling in love with 71–6
    game 240
    jam 119–20
    leftovers 151
    nuts 250–1, 252–3

potatoes 269
prunes 174
pumpkin and squash 225
salad dressings 19–20
salt cod 59
Sunday lunch 115–16
violets 94
Franco, Francisco 29, 30
frisée 274
Friuli-Venezia Giulia 256–7
fungi 242–3

**G**
gages 173
game 239–41
garlic 19, 23–4, 25
garnishes 204
Genoa 256
Georgia 220–1, 235, 251, 271
    blackberries 279–80
    herbs 156, 157, 159, 161
Gide, André 207
ginger 46–7, 256, 259
Goldstein, Joyce 125, 126, 127
Gopnik, Adam 54, 55
granitas 39, 92
grapefruit 39
Gray, Dr Annie 130–1
Greco, El 28, 31
Greece 85, 157, 159
    fruit 208–9, 212–13
    herbs 161
    pomegranates 212–13
    yogurt 83
greengages 173
gremolata 41
grouse 240, 241
Gulati, Roopa 167–8, 169

**H**
Hallowe'en 217–18, 223
hams 231
haricot (navy) beans 234
harissa 47
Hartley, Dorothy 280
hazelnuts 249–50, 263, 266
Heaney, Seamus 261, 279
herbs 63–70, 155–62, 255, 259
high tea 165

horseradish 256, 257
Hughes, Ted 30, 31
Hungary 172, 234
    nuts 253
    spices 47, 258, 256, 259
    vegetables 269, 271
*hüzün* 102

**I**
'ice in heaven' 15
India 167–70, 256
Iran 83, 157, 187, 188, 255
Istanbul 97–103
Italy 37, 109–14, 142
    beans 234
    bread 188, 190
    cheese 284–6
    nuts 250, 251, 252, 253
    pasta 105
    Piedmont 261–6, 285
    ricotta 87
    salt cod 59
    spices 256–7
    truffles 263–6
    vegetables 225, 269, 273

**J**
jam 119–21, 153, 173
Japanese food 193–6
Jefferson, Thomas 149
Jerusalem artichokes 270
juniper 258

**K**
Kahlo, Frida 182
Kettilby, Mary 290

**L**
labneh 84, 85
lamb 45, 152
Lamothe-en-Blaisy 72–3
lavender 68–9
Lawrence, DH 207
*le grand aïoli* 24
Lebanon 158, 187
leeks 272–3
leftovers 151–3
lemons 39–41
lentils 236–7

# INDEX

Les Vapeurs 74–5
lettuce 140, 274
lingonberries 277–8
López-Alt, J Kenji 236
Lorca, Federico García 28, 29
Loren, Sophia 106, 107
Lot Valley 245–8
Lough Neagh 299, 300
Luis 28
lunches 139

## M

McCullers, Carson 149
McGee, Harold 162
Machado, Antonio 28, 29
Madrid 27–9, 31–2
main courses 139
Maison Premiere 309
Mallorca 35–6
mango chutney 168
maple syrup 293–7
Maria Carolina de Bourbon 111
Marie-Antoinette 111
marinades 84–5
marjoram 65
Markham, Gervase 166
marmalade 289–91
Matuchet, Monsieur 246–8
May, Robert 166
mayonnaise 24–5
Medici family 37
Mediterranean 57–8, 65, 125
Mehmed II, Sultan 100
membrillo 210–11
menus 123–7, 135–42
Mexico 181–3, 225
Meyer, Danny 306
mezze 139, 140, 219
Middle East 85, 99, 220
    bread 186, 192
    fruit 208–9, 213–14
    herbs and spices 47, 156–7, 159, 160–1
    rose water 91, 93
    yogurt 82–3
milk pudding 101
Minetta Tavern 308–9
mint 155–6, 157, 160–1
molasses 294–5
Molokhovets, Elena 220

Morocco 37, 141
    bread 188
    ginger 46, 47
    herbs and spices 44, 48–9, 94, 158, 160, 161, 256
Morrison, Van 299
mushrooms 242–3

## N

Naples 110–11, 113–14
Napoleon 90
Native Americans 148, 276, 294
New York 303–10
Normandy 74, 285
North Africa 41, 91, 99, 133, 158
Northern Ireland 216, 299, 304
Norway 272, 287
nuts 249–53, 263

## O

Oaxaca 182–3
October 215–18
oil pickles 168
olive oil 19–20, 22–4, 60, 263
olives 20–2, 32
orange blossom 14, 90, 95
orange flower water 91, 92, 93–4
oranges 35–9, 42, 65, 112
    marmalade 289–91
oregano 64, 65–6, 67
Ottoman Empire 99, 100

## P

*pa amb oli* 21
Pamuk, Orhan 102
panzanella 134
paprika 47, 258, 259
parsley 155, 156–7, 158, 161
parsnips 269
pasta 105–7, 112
Pavese, Cesare 261
Paz 29, 30–1
peaches 142
'pearl diver's rice' 15
pears 200–2
pecans 251–2
Persephone 212
Persians 44, 90, 160, 161
Peter the Great 219

315

pheasant 240, 241
*piadina* 190–1
piccalilli 166
pickles 41–2, 147, 148, 165–70, 175
Piedmont 261–6, 285
pigs 228–30
pilaf 83, 99, 152, 157, 160
*pimentón* 47
Plath, Sylvia 31
Pliny 160–1
plums 152–3, 171–3, 175
Poilâne, Apollonia 130
Poland 172, 175, 271, 281
pomegranate molasses 213–14
pomegranates 207, 212–14
Poorandokht, Queen 83
poppy seeds 257
pork 227–31
Portugal 37, 290, 301
    cumin 49
    herbs 159
    salt cod 58, 59
potatoes 152, 269
preservation 147–9
Pritchett, VS 27
Provence 63, 67, 68
prunes 174–6
puddings 138, 140
Puglia 110, 112
pumpkins 223–6
purple-sprouting broccoli 272

Q
quail 240–1
quince 207, 209–10, 285, 290

R
rabbit 174, 175, 240, 241
radicchio 273
ras al hanout 91
Ravello 109, 110
red kidney beans 235
Renaissance painters 37
Renoir, Pierre Auguste 20–1
Republic of Ireland 30, 299–300
ricotta 86–7, 113
*rigani* 66
Rikyū, Sen no 195–6
Rivera, Diego 182
Rockwell, Norman 52

Roden, Claudia 14, 91–2
Rodgers, Judy 125
Rogers, Richard 33
Rohmer, Éric 73
Romans 90–1, 210
Rome 105–6
rose petals 89, 90, 91, 92, 93, 95
rose water 91, 92, 93, 94
rosehips 280, 281
rosemary 64–5, 67
Rosenzweig, Annie 306
Russia 53, 256, 281
    fruit 172, 175, 278
    vegetables 269, 271–2
    *zakuski* table 219–21

S
*sabzi khordan* 156–7
saffron 43–4, 45, 47
salad dressings 19, 26
salads 139–40, 280
salmon 157, 217, 256, 300
*salmoriglio* 66
salt cod 57, 58–9
salt cravings 57–61
San Francisco 125, 126, 127, 130
Scandinavia 255, 256
    cheese 287
    rosehips 280–1
    soured cream 259–60
    vegetables 269, 270
Schneider, Romy 71, 72
Scotland 291
senses 15–16
Seville 31
sharbats 91–2
Sicily 110
    herbs 66, 160
    oranges 37, 38, 49, 112
    ricotta 86, 113
Singh, Dharamjit 169
sloes 281–2
Smith, Delia 78
smörgåsbord 219, 256
*socca* 191
Solana, José Gutiérrez 31
sorbets 39, 92
Sorenson, Irene 275
soup 139, 152, 203–5, 225–6
soured cream 259–60

# INDEX

sourdough 129, 130, 133
Spain 27–33, 75, 141
    membrillo 210–11
    oranges 37
    salt cod 58
    spices 44, 49
spices 43–9, 91, 255–9
Square One 125
squash 223–6
starters 139
stock 152, 203–4
Stockholm 256
sugar-on-snow parties 294, 297
Sugiura, Yuki 194–5
summer's end 163–4
Sunday lunch 115–17
swede 271
Sweden 256, 270, 280–1, 287
Switzerland 285–6

## T
tabbouleh 158
table, around the 51–5
tapas 139, 219
tapenade 21–2
tarragon 156–7
thyme 67–8
toast 129–31
*tonir* 188
*trasnochar* 32
Traunfeld, Jerry 92
Tree Top 35
Truffaut, François 73
truffles 263–6
Turkey 83, 85, 97–103, 157, 255
turnips 217, 271

## U
Umu 193–4
Ungerer, Tomi 228
Union Square Café 306
United States of America 163, 164, 217
    beans 234
    blackberries 279
    cranberries 275–7
    maple syrup 293–7
    nuts 251
    preserved foods 147–9
    pumpkin and squash 225

## V
Van Gogh, Vincent 20
vegetables, winter 268–74
Venice 256–7
venison 241
Vermont 148, 293–7
*vin d'orange* 178
vinaigrettes 42, 72, 140
*vins maisons* 178–9
violets 89–90, 94–5
Virgin Mary 37, 58

## W
walnuts 249, 250–1
Waters, Alice 123–4, 126, 127, 137, 147
Wells, Patricia 74, 245
Wells, Pete 309
wild produce 239–43
Wilder, Laura Ingalls 148, 226, 293–4, 297
Wilson, C Anne 290
winter cooking 223–7
Wolfert, Paula 247
Wood, Willis 295–6

## Y
yogurt 81–4, 87

## Z
Zabar 306
*zakuski* table 219–21
Zuni Café 125

# ACKNOWLEDGEMENTS

Huge thanks to my editor, Lucy Bannell, who is a tireless perfectionist. We spent days together pulling this book into shape. And to Chad Worsley, the producer of the audio version, who guided me from rookie to performer.

Matt Cox has produced a beautiful, spare design and discovered the artist, Vivienne Williams, to work on the cover. We knew immediately that she was the right person. Thank you for being part of this project, Vivienne.

Thanks also to Charlotte Sanders, Matthew Grindon and Claire Scott for arranging my publicity tour, the interviews, podcasts and anything that required technical skill (because I don't have any). Charlotte, you are the very best travel companion. Özlem Warren, thanks so much for your help with Turkish pronounciation.

Thank you to my publisher, Alison Starling, who was endlessly enthusiastic and patient even when I wanted to change just one more thing. Ellen Sleath collected the pieces that formed the beginnings of *Around the Table* by going through twenty-five years of my writing (for which she deserves some kind of medal).

This is dedicated to Claudia Roden, who, since I bought *The Book of Middle Eastern Food* decades ago, has shown me what food writing can be.